DATE DUE

Elder Tales

*Stories of Wisdom and Courage
from Around the World*

Dan Keding

**LIBRARIES
UNLIMITED**

A Member of the Greenwood Publishing Group

Westport, Connecticut • London

Library of Congress Cataloging-in-Publication Data

Keding, Dan.
  Elder tales : stories of wisdom and courage from around the world / Dan Keding.
    p. cm.
  Includes bibliographical references and index.
  ISBN 978-1-59158-594-7 (alk. paper)
  1. Older people—Folklore. 2. Aging—Folklore. I. Title.
GR452.K43 2008
808.8'0354—dc22   2007029081

British Library Cataloguing in Publication Data is available.

Library of Congress Catalog Card Number: 2007029081
ISBN: 978-1-59158-594-7

First published in 2008

Libraries Unlimited, 88 Post Road West, Westport, CT 06881
A Member of the Greenwood Publishing Group, Inc.
www.lu.com

Printed in the United States of America

∞™

The paper used in this book complies with the
Permanent Paper Standard issued by the National
Information Standards Organization (Z39.48–1984).

10   9   8   7   6   5   4   3   2   1

I wish to dedicate this book to my wife, Ann Tandy Lacy, who has encouraged me and understands why I do what I do.

I wish also to dedicate it to all the elders who have touched my life, including Ann Keding, Sara Lee Thorpe, Hillard Thorpe, Frank Lacy, and Art Thieme. I hope that I can follow your example.

Contents

Preface

The stories I have gathered here, except for two, are all my own retellings of traditional folktales. I have kept the intent, the place, and the cultural background as close to the original as possible. What I have done is to present the stories in a more user-friendly, teller-friendly way. Sometimes this meant untangling a story from the web of a well-meaning folklorist's language, sometimes it meant finding several versions to find missing pieces that would contribute to a more continuous flow, sometimes it meant rewriting a passage to make an easier transition for the would be teller and his or her audience. I have tried to give sources whenever it was possible and provide enough information that the reader—especially the storyteller, teacher, librarian, nursing home or elder center worker—would be able to find other versions that might be more to their liking or that might reflect their own or their clients cultural background.

I want to thank my wife Tandy Lacy for all her editorial skills and her tireless reading of my stories. She always asks the questions that make everything clear to me. Also, a thank you to Dovie Thomason for sending me the wonderful story "Beaver Woman and Eagle" and to Tam Dang Wei for giving me permission to include her sweet story, "The Elephant's Gratitude."

Thanks to Barbara Ittner at Libraries Unlimited for her faith in this project and her continued support.

Introduction

I grew up with an "elder" in my house. My grandmother, Rose Culap, was an everyday part of my life as a child. It was from her that I learned to love story as a spoken, oral tradition. From my mother, Ann Keding, and my aunt, Mary Culap, I learned the story of the written word with books on King Arthur, Robin Hood, and classic children's literature. The wisdom that I learned from the traditional stories of my grandmother and the literary influences of her daughters wove a spell on me that resulted years later in my decision to become a storyteller. One can never discount the importance of elders in our lives.

From my grandmother's stories I learned about wisdom, heroism, choices, responsibility, foolishness, and all the other lessons that we now try to pour into our children's heads through abstract contrivances thought up by well-meaning psychologists. The importance of our elders lies in their ability to inform us of who we are by telling us where we came from in the first place. By giving us a cultural starting point, our elders are able to give us the knowledge and tools we need to approach adulthood and eventually our own roles as family and community elders.

The place of the elder in our society is not the revered one that it was so long ago when the knowledge held in the minds of each elder was the knowledge that would allow their communities to survive. Even today, these simple stories help us understand that we are not alone, that others have felt as we feel, cried and laughed, buried their dead and raised their children, and dreamed the dreams that needed to be dreamed.

Now we seem to think it quaint when we get advice from an older parent, grandparent, or uncle or aunt. We smile—if not outwardly, then inwardly—and wonder what knowledge could they possibly possess that we don't know, already have, or might ever need in this rapidly changing twenty-first century. Even in this age of computers and instant knowledge, we all lack the one thing our elders will always have—experience. Experience in living, dealing with others, facing fears, growing up, and, finally, facing the end of our time. These are lessons that cannot be taught by computer, DVD, CD—or any electronic device. We look into the eyes of our elders and we see something that we can never see in the mirror; we see our future.

Elders in today's society are too often measured against the values of our "youth culture"—physical strength and agility, sex appeal, and the myth of eternal youth. The stories in this book demonstrate what elders have to offer—humor, wisdom, and experience. This collection is meant to give educators, storytellers, and general readers a wealth of material on elders for young and old alike. The stories can be used to incorporate themes of old age into any program; or they can be used for an entire program based on elders. Stories may be read aloud, retold, or simply read silently. Students can use the stories for research and reports on cultural traditions, the various challenges each generation faces, and the power of the oral tradition. Educators and storytellers who work in schools or public libraries will find suggestions for using the stories both as they are and as a starting point for other related projects provided at the back of this book. Those who work with senior populations (e.g., at senior centers or nursing homes) will find a number of suggestions for discussions and activities with seniors. However they are used, it is hoped that the stories will encourage a broader understanding and deeper appreciation of elders including their varied and vital roles in our history and in our future in those who tell or read or listen to these stories.

The stories in this book come from around the world, and they show elders in as many roles as possible—from the noble Beowulf to the foolish, but oddly wise Nasrudin. We often discount the role of older people as heroes, but in this collection you will find senior swashbucklers and quiet heroes alike. Serious tales of knowledge are side by side with trickster tales—both a kind of wisdom that should not be taken for granted. Included are stories about elders in their family life and in the animal kingdom, tales of magic along with stories about justice coming about in spite of itself. There is even a section of stories especially for elders that bring some serious topics to light through humor. For each story in the collection, I cite another source—usually a unique retelling or favorite version of mine, but my retellings are based on a variety of sources, some of them oral. Most of the stories here are available in many different versions from many different cultures and nations. An extensive bibliography is provided to help you explore these versions and other stories that will open up more possibilities.

There is wisdom in these tales, but it is only the beginning. Seek out the elders in your family, your community, your profession, your art and find more wisdom than you ever imagined.

I hope you find reading this book is as enlightening to you, as telling these stories is to me.

Chapter One

Wisdom

The King and the Peasant

Poland

As the sun was getting low in the sky, old Matthias straightened his back and looked toward his cottage. It was time to go home and end his day of hard work in the fields. As he glanced toward the road, he saw a cloud of dust that gradually took the form of a troop of men riding toward the city. At their head, rode the king, leading his lords and knights home after a day of hunting in the nearby woods. The fading sun glittered off of the crown that circled the king's head. Suddenly, much to the old man's surprise, the company came to a halt. The king and three other men turned their horses toward Matthias, coming to a stop right in front of the old man, who now knelt, head bowed in front of his ruler.

"Arise, old friend," said the king, "and tell me, why did you not rise early enough to finish your work?"

Matthias replied, "I did, my gracious and beloved king, but God did not allow me."

The king nodded, and then asked, "How long has that snowy orchard been blooming on that sage mountain top?"

Matthias smiled, "Going on forty years, my good lord."

The king nodded his head, as if he understood every word the old man spoke. "Tell me, how many years have the streams been flowing from under the mountain?"

"The streams, my lord, have been flowing and flowing for fifteen years now."

"So far, so good, my friend." The king looked pleased. "Now one more thing, when the three geese come from the east, will you be able to fleece them?"

The old peasant looked up at the king and smiled, "They will be well fleeced, my king."

The king smiled back at the old man, then he undid a golden belt that ringed his own waist and handed to the Matthias. He thanked him for his words and hoped that God would see fit to bless them both. The king and his three counselors turned and rode back to the waiting company, continuing their journey to the palace.

Later that evening, the king called the three advisors who had witnessed his conversation with Matthias to his chambers. He asked the men to explain the meaning of his questions and the old man's answers

The three men thought for a long time, trying to explain the riddles, but none even came close to their true meaning. Finally, the king told them that they had thirty days to figure out the meaning of the conversation. If they failed, he warned, he would replace them with new counselors.

Day after day, night after night, the three men debated the meaning of the words spoken by the king and the peasant. They repeated the words over and over again, trying to find a clue, but to no avail. Finally, they decided that only one person could help them, so they visited old Matthias.

The old man welcomed the king's counselors into his home, but he refused to enlighten them upon the meaning of his conversation with the king. The three men pleaded and threatened, but it was useless. He would not be moved. Finally, each man put a bag of one hundred gold coins on the table. Matthias smiled, gathered the bags into his arms, and disappeared with them into his back room. He then came back and told the three counselors what the conversation was all about.

"The king asked, with his first question, why I did not marry young and have sons and daughters to work my fields. I replied that I did, but that God had taken them and that all my children had died before me. Next the king asked how long ago my hair had turned white. I told him forty years. The third question was how long had I grieved for my beloved wife and I answered that I had cried fifteen years now, in her remembrance." Matthias stopped and smiled at the looks of profound amazement that had come across the faces of the three men.

"Lastly, the king asked if I would fleece the three foolish geese that came from the east. Those geese are the three of you, gentlemen, and by taking your gold to explain my conversation with the king, I have fleeced you well indeed."

The three men left the cottage, poorer in coin but richer in wisdom for having met the truly wise old Matthias.

This is a story I heard as a boy from a neighbor. Humor and wisdom really do go hand in hand. There is a great version in the book Ride with the Sun: An Anthology of Folk Tales & Stories *from the United Nations, edited by Harold Courlander.*

Fence Post Wisdom

United States

Wisdom can be found about anywhere, anytime, all you have to do is be patient, keep your mouth shut, and your eyes and your ears open. At the turn of the century (I mean the one in 1900, not the more recent one), small towns had general stores that not only sold the folks anything they needed but also supplied all the news they needed, too. This was the place to catch up on what was going on in town if you lived on the farm and what was happening in the country if you lived in town. This was the gathering place, the center of the town.

On the front porch of one such general store, there was a heated argument going on between some farmers on the longevity of fence post woods. Now these farmers were equally divided in their opinion on the natural durability of white oak versus chestnut. During the whole exchange, the store owner, a venerable and respected elder in this community, who had farmed in his youth and had run this store for the last forty years, just sat in his rocking chair keeping his peace and listening to their debate. After almost an hour of back and forth good-natured jawing, the farmers decided to ask old Tom what he thought about this thorny issue.

"Now," one man asked, "what do you think, Tom? Which last longer for fence posts, white oak or chestnut?"

Tom rocked his chair just a tad slower, closed his eyes, and seemed to study the situation internally. After what seemed a very long time, and oddly enough, was a very long time, he opened his eyes, stopped his rocking, and turned to the farmers, who had kept a silent vigil during this entire meditative process.

"Oak lasts longer." He spoke with the conviction of ancient wisdom and studied examination.

One farmer was not to be denied further benefit of Tom's expertise.

"By how long, Tom?"

Tom rocked his chair a bit faster and closed his eyes and furrowed his brow in contemplation. The farmers again stood in silent admiration of this wise old man and leaned forward so as not to miss a word. After another long stretch, Tom stopped rocking and spoke.

"About twenty minutes."

Wisdom, all you need is the patience to receive it.

I'm not sure when I first heard this story, but I know it was when I was a very young folk singer in the early seventies. It may have been told by that great raconteur and folksinger Art Thieme, but I'm not quite sure.

Art sure does have great stories and his delivery is always the best. I have heard many versions since from old-timers and storytellers alike.

The Monks and the Geisha

Japan

Once, a long time ago, two monks were traveling from Kyoto to Edo. As they walked, they talked about meditation and prayer and their search for life's meaning. The rainy day turned sunny as their conversation became more intense.

As they turned the bend in the road, they saw a geisha standing there by the side of the pathway. She was beautiful, clothed in a silk kimono and carrying an umbrella to shield her from the noon sun.

As they approached, she turned to them and asked if one of them would help her by carrying her across the muddy road. She was afraid she would ruin her beautiful clothes.

The younger monk turned away from her without even offering a reply. But the older man bowed graciously and, sweeping her up in his arms, carried her across the muddy highway. She thanked him and they bowed in farewell.

The younger monk seethed with anger and scarcely spoke for the rest of the day to the older man. As night approached, they sought a bed and meal at a local monastery. As they finally laid their heads down to fall asleep, the young man exploded. "How could you look, let alone touch that woman? We are forbidden any contact with a woman like that one."

The older man looked at the younger monk with a smile that was sly and also a bit melancholy. "I left that woman back down the road. Why are you still carrying her around?"

I sometimes feel as if I've known this story forever. I don't remember when I first heard it, but it has been a story that I just seem to have known forever. It can be found in the wonderful book Zen Flesh, Zen Bones. *It has a different name, but I won't tell you—read the whole book. It's one of my favorite books; I've worn out several copies over the years.*

In Your Hands

Jewish

Once there was a young rabbi who settled down in a community. He was eager to teach and make his mark in the world. After several months he had been invited to speak at the local temple and had taught a few students, but felt he was still in the shadow of the old rabbi who had been there for many years. The students flocked to learn from this old man and the young man had no followers at all.

The young man knew that the only way to attract students was to discredit the old rabbi in front of all his students. The young man thought about it for many nights until at last he devised a plan. He decided to approach the old teacher during his morning lesson. The young rabbi would keep a live dove in his hand, behind his back. Then he would ask the old man if the bird he was holding was alive or dead. If the old man said dead, the young rabbi would let the dove fly free; if the old man said alive, the young man would break the bird's neck with his fingers and present a dead bird to him. The young rabbi's plan was foolproof. There was no way for the old teacher to win this contest. This would finally prove that the old man was not as wise as the people in the community thought.

The morning came and, as the old man and his students sat in the shade of a huge tree, the young man approached. The young rabbi waited for just the right moment, and then he stood up and spoke.

"Rabbi," he started, "I have in my hand a bird. Is it alive or dead?"

The old man looked up at him with a face that was serene, but also a bit sad. "That, my friend, is entirely up to you," he said.

The young rabbi stood there for a moment. Finally, he let the bird go and sat down at the feet of the old man.

This wonderful story can be found in collections from many parts of the world. A version can be found in Stories of the Spirit, Stories of the Heart *by Christina Feldman and Jack Kornfield. There is also a wonderful version from Africa titled* Why Monkeys Live in Trees & Other Stories from Benin *by Raouf Mama.*

The Mountain Where Old People Were Abandoned

Japan

A long time ago, there was a lord who commanded that when people reached old age they should be taken to a mountain canyon and left there to die. He felt that once they became too old to work in the fields or ply their trade, they were no longer useful. In a nearby village, there was a young farmer whose father had now reached the age of abandonment and, since the lord had commanded it, the son now took his father on his back to the mountain to be left there to die. They walked deeper and deeper into the wilderness and, as they went along, the old man broke the tips off of branches in order to mark the trail.

"Father, why do you break the branches off? Is it to mark the trail and find your way home again?"

"No, my son, it is not for me that I mark the trail, but for you. I know that I cannot return, but I am afraid that you will become lost on your way home and I would be grief stricken if anything happened to you on my account."

When the young farmer heard these words, he thought back on how kind and wise his father had always been and how he had tried his best throughout the years to guide his son along life's journey. Stopping for a moment, the son shifted his father's weight on his back and then turned around and walked back home. By day, he hid his father under the porch and at night, he brought the aged man into the house and fed and cared for him.

Now, the lord of that land was a man of whims who would often taunt his subjects by asking them to undertake challenging and sometimes ridiculous tasks. One day, he gathered the farmers from the region and said, "You must each bring me a rope woven from ashes."

All the farmers were very troubled, knowing the impossibility of the request. The young farmer went home and told his father of the lord's command as they ate their evening meal. "A rope of ash is what he wants. How can I do this?"

"You must weave a rope very tightly then burn it and bring it carefully to the lord."

The young man was amazed and overjoyed at his father's advice and quickly went about his task. The next day, he was the only one who brought an ashen rope to the lord. The lord was pleased and praised the young man for his quick thinking.

Next, the lord commanded, "Each of you must bring a conch shell with a thread passed through it."

Once again, the young farmer sought out his father's wisdom. The old man smiled and said, "Take a conch shell and point the tip to the light. Take a thread and stick a grain of rice on it. Then give the rice to an ant and make it crawl into the shell. The ant will make its way toward the light and weave the thread through the chambers of the shell."

Once more, the young farmer was the only one who was able to complete the task and again, the lord was pleased. "How were you able to come up with a way to solve the riddles of these tasks and complete them so well?"

The young farmer took a deep breath and answered the lord. "I love my father very much and when it came time to take him to the mountain canyon to die I could not bear it. He was always so wise and kind. Instead, I brought him back to my house and hid him there by day and fed and cared for him at night. I asked him about these problems and he quickly solved them both."

When the lord heard this, he was impressed with the young man's devotion and the old man's wisdom. He knew now that it was a mistake to lose all that knowledge, so he commanded that the practice of abandonment cease and that old people should be revered and honored.

And so it was and so it should be.

This is a well-known story from Japan that can be found in many collections and in other cultures. You can find a version in Keigo Seki's book Folktales of Japan, *originally published by the University of Chicago Press.*

The Wise Old Weaver

Turkey

One day, the padishah was looking out over his capital city from the balcony of his palace when he saw a flag waving back and forth above a tiny house. He could not identify the flag, so he ordered one of his servants to go and find out about it. The servant found the house and knocked on the door. An old man answered and invited the padishah's servant to come in.

The old man was a weaver and he sat down at his loom and returned to his work while he and the servant spoke. Looking down, the servant saw that the cuffs of the man's trousers were muddy and soiled.

"Why don't you clean the mud off your pants?" he asked.

The old man smiled. "You see, over there in the corner?" he asked, pointing to a dark spot in the earthen floor. I fill those holes, but the rats keep digging new ones, so I mix the clay mud with my feet while I sit at my loom. Later, when I get up, I fill the holes."

"That is a wonderful way to save time," remarked the servant. "And what is that pole sticking up through the roof of your house?"

"The pole has a flag on its end," replied the weaver. "By waving the flag, I am able to keep the birds away from the wheat my wife has placed on the roof to dry. The pole is attached to the loom and moves back and forth as I weave, keeping the birds frightened enough to stay away from our roof."

The palace servant was amazed by the man's genius. "Why is there a string tied to your wrist?" he asked.

The string is attached to my child's cradle so my wife can have time to wash herself and have a moment's peace. I can attend the baby while I work, by rocking the child to sleep as my hand moves across the loom."

"And tell me, who are those children sitting at the window across from you, reading books?"

"Those are my neighbors' children. I teach them while I work here," replied the modest weaver.

The servant was very impressed with a man who could carry on five tasks at one time. He thanked the weaver and made his way back to the palace to report to the padishah.

The padishah was so impressed when he heard the story that he sent his servant back to the weaver to invite him to work in the palace as an advisor. The servant delivered the note and the old man and his family came to live at the palace.

Not long afterward, a fierce-looking stranger was admitted into the palace courtyard. The man dismounted from his horse and sat down inside of a circle he drew in the middle of the courtyard—all the while glaring at everyone fiercely and not saying a word.

Many of the padishah's advisers tried to speak to the man, but he just stared straight ahead and said nothing. Finally, the ruler called for the old weaver to come and figure out this riddle for him. The padishah asked the weaver if he could make the man talk or if he could at least try to find meaning in this bizarre behavior.

The weaver went to the hen house and got a small rooster and put it under his arm. Then he asked his wife to bring their young son to him. When the boy was brought, the weaver went to the courtyard to meet the stranger. The padishah had a fine carpet laid out at the edge of the courtyard so he could sit to watch the weaver and the stranger.

The old weaver walked into the circle the stranger had made, and, taking a stick, he made a smaller circle and sat down inside it. The stranger reached into his pocket and drew out a handful of millet and scattered it around the inside of the two circles. The weaver then took the rooster that he had hidden in the folds of his long robe and placed it down in the circle where it began to eat the millet hungrily. When the stranger saw this he cried, "But there will be bloodshed." When the weaver heard these words, he placed his young son on the ground inside of the circle. When the stranger saw the child he bowed his head to the weaver, jumped on his horse, and galloped away. As soon as this happened the weaver called to his wife, and he and his family returned to their quarters in the palace.

The padishah was totally puzzled by this whole exchange and was so curious that he ordered the weaver back to his courtyard to explain what the ruler and all the members of his court had just witnessed.

"Your majesty, the stranger was a Muscovite, an ambassador from the Tsar," explained the weaver. "By drawing a circle and sitting in it, he was saying that the world was owned by the Tsar. By drawing a circle inside his and sitting in it, I was saying that we are a great nation, too, and we have a right to occupy part of the world. When he scattered the seed on the ground, he was telling me that Russia has many soldiers. When I put the rooster down and it started eating the seeds, I was saying that we have many heroes who can defeat his armies.

When he said, "But there will be bloodshed," I put my child down in the circle telling him that I would wager the life of my child on the outcome of such a war."

The padishah was so impressed that he offered the weaver any gift he wanted. The old man replied, "I am a weaver. This and the small service that I do your majesty is all the thanks I need. May you have good health for all the days of your life." The weaver smiled and returned to his loom, always ready to help his ruler whenever needed.

This tale from Turkey, shares the argument without words found in the story "A Debate in Sign Language." There is a longer, wonderful version found in Tales Alive in Turkey *by Warren Walker and Ahmet Uysal.*

The Storyteller and the Samurai

Japan

M any years ago, there was an old storyteller—a master of his art—making his way through the countryside. As the sun lowered in the sky, he knew, from the grumbling in his stomach and the aching in his bones, that he needed to find a place to rest that evening and, even more importantly, a meal. His prayers would soon be answered, for there at the foot of the hill was a dojo, a school of swordsmanship where young, aspiring samurai could study under a master swordsman. The custom in those ancient days was to earn a meal and lodging for the night by engaging one of the students in a duel using wooden swords. The old man looked thoughtfully at the dojo and then felt the age in his bones and the weariness in his muscles and knew what a duel would mean to a man of his years. After a moment, a smile crossed his lips and he walked to the door of the school and knocked.

A young swordsman answered the door. "Grandfather, what can I do for you tonight?"

The old man smiled and said, "I am here to challenge the master of this school."

The young man laughed and said, "Grandfather, why don't you challenge one of our first year students?"

"No, I am here to challenge the master."

"Why not one of our second year students?"

"No, I insist on meeting the master in a duel."

The old man was brought into the training hall where all the students looked on with curiosity at this frail, old storyteller who had challenged their teacher. You see to challenge the master, a samurai, was to fight a duel with swords of steel, a duel to the death.

Word was sent to the master of the school, a swordsman whose reputation was known throughout Japan. He came to the hall and bowed to the storyteller. At his side, in his obi, he carried the long sword, the katana of the samurai. He signaled for one of his students to hand a sword to the old storyteller. The storyteller placed the katana on the floor in front of him and never glanced at it again.

The master of the school finally spoke. "I accept your challenge. Please take up your weapon and we shall begin."

Slowly, the swordsman drew his sword to strike. As this happened, the old man finally spoke.

"Once, a long time ago, there was a small village near a beautiful stream at the foot of a mighty mountain. At the end of the village there was a cottage where an old man lived. Every day he would go to the stream and listen as the fish told him the stories of the places they had traveled, the people they had seen, and the stories they had heard on their journey. Then the old man would go to the village and tell his friends his new stories as they drank their morning tea. This ..."

As the old storyteller was speaking, the master of the school lowered his sword and bowed. "You have defeated me," he said to the weary traveler.

The students shouted. "How could he have won? He never struck a blow. He never even picked up a sword."

The samurai turned and looked at them and smiled. "How many times have I told you that to win in battle you must stay in the present, you must stay in the moment. This man took me to a place far away and long ago. He could have slain me at will."

And so it was and so it will be for all those who tell tales and stories from their heart, and all those who listen.

This story is very popular in the more traditional dojos *that study Japanese martial arts. I've told it to many an eager student in* iaido *(Japanese sword art) hoping to impart the wisdom I've gained from it. I first heard it told in Japan among a group of* iaido *practitioners.*

Chapter Two

Tricksters

The Old Woman Who Outwitted Death

Hungary

Once upon a time, whether true or not, I cannot say, there was an old, old woman. She was older than the gardener who planted the first tree, yet she was full of life, full of wisdom, and never dreamed that death might someday pass her way. She washed her clothes and scrubbed her cottage; she cooked her meals and baked her breads; she planted her garden and tended her flowers. She was kind to strangers and was loved by her neighbors. She was busy with life.

One day, Death remembered the old woman and came knocking on her cottage door. When she saw who he was she told him she couldn't possibly leave that day. She had just started her laundry and she needed to rinse the clothes, hang them on the line, and then iron them when they were dry. No, but she might be ready by the next morning, if death would be so kind as to return then.

Since Death had forgotten about her so many times, he thought it only fair to give her another day to get her life in order. "You can expect me at the same time tomorrow." As he walked out of her garden, he took some chalk from his pocket and wrote the word "tomorrow" on the gatepost.

The next day he returned and told her that she must come along, that he didn't have all day.

The old woman smiled and said, "But my dear Death, you must be mistaken. This is not the day you were to come, just look and see what you wrote on my gatepost. That's when you are to come for me."

Death looked at the gatepost and sure enough there was a word in his own writing, "Tomorrow."

"There," said the old woman. "You must come for me tomorrow."

So, Death went away and returned the next day. The old woman was standing by the door, waiting. "Death, don't you remember what you wrote on the gatepost? You aren't coming for me today, but tomorrow."

And so it went on for an entire month.

Finally, Death had had enough of this game. "Old woman, you have been cheating me. Tomorrow is your last day and I will be coming for you then." As he walked out of her garden he rubbed the word "tomorrow" off the gatepost.

The old woman stopped smiling. She tried to think of a way to stop Death from taking her, but she didn't have any ideas left. That night she tossed and turned and didn't sleep at all.

In the morning, the old woman decided she would hide in the honey barrel that she kept in the corner of her kitchen. She eased herself down into the thick, rich, golden-colored honey, leaving only her nose and eyes above the rim to watch for Death. But then she realized that Death would look for her and thought that this might be the very first place he would try. So, she climbed out of the honey barrel and quickly hid in a chest full of the goose feathers that she had been saving to make a nice comforter. But, just as she settled herself in the feathers, she wondered if Death would open the chest, so she slowly climbed out and began to walk across the room to the stairs that led to the attic. Just then Death walked through the door.

He glanced around but didn't see the old woman anywhere. Instead, he spied this strange creature, all covered with white feathers and something thick, slimy and golden that seemed to ooze from it. It wasn't a bird and it wasn't a person. It was a horrible sight.

Death was so terrified that he turned and ran from the old woman's house, never to return. The old woman cleaned herself up and once more got busy with life.

––––––––––––––––––

This is a lovely story of Death being fooled by a mortal. I guess a good disguise is all you need. You can find a version in the Fairy Tale Tree *by Vladislav Stanovsky and Jan Vladislav.*

The Deluded Dragon

Eastern European (Romany)

A long time ago, there was an old man who had a large family, far too large to feed and clothe and house. He lived with his wife and their many children deep in the middle of the forest, sheltered in a small hovel, nothing more than a hole in the ground with a roof of branches.

One day the poor old man asked his wife to make him a honey cake for his dinner and then set off to find some work and make a little money to buy food. He walked all morning until he came to a well. Beside the well there was a large stone that served as a table for travelers. The old man sat next to the stone and placed his honey cake on it, thinking he would eat the cake after he had rested a bit. Soon, he was fast asleep. While he slept the birds came down and gobbled up his honey cake, and when he woke the flies were finishing the crumbs.

"Leave me nothing," he cried when he saw the flies. Quickly, he brought his hand down on the stone killing fifty of his tormentors with one blow. Proud of this feat, he took a burnt stick and wrote on the stone table that he had killed fifty souls with just one blow. Then, still tired and hungry, he put his head down and resumed his nap.

While the old man slept, a dragon came to the well for a drink. When he saw the man sleeping there, the dragon crept closer. Reading what was written on the stone, the dragon stepped back in fright. Feeling the ground shake, the old man woke up and saw the dragon. Then the man was frightened, so he and the dragon just sat there, staring at each other.

Each one was so afraid of the other that together they swore an oath of brotherhood. They would be friends no matter what happened, and neither one would harm the other. The dragon then invited the old man to his palace to dine with him and his wife. As the old man walked down the forest path, the dragon followed. Each time the dragon exhaled, his breath pushed the old man forward, and each time the dragon inhaled he pulled the old man backward.

The dragon was perplexed by this behavior. "Brother, why do you walk running forward and then running backward?"

The old man replied, "Brother, when I think I might kill you, I run backward, but when I remember our oath, I run forward. Perhaps you should walk in front, so I can keep my eyes on you and remember my promise to be your brother."

The dragon was afraid that the old man might kill him, so he replied, "I will gladly walk in front of you."

Soon, they came to a cherry tree filled with the ripest, most delicious-tasting cherries. The dragon flew up to the top branches and began to eat. He looked down at the old man and said, "Brother, come up here. The nearer they are to the sun, the sweeter they taste."

"No, thank you. I can reach these lower branches where the birds do not peck away all the juice as they do further up the tree."

The dragon took hold of a huge branch filled with cherries and bent it down so it touched the ground. "Here brother, these are the best cherries of all. Take hold of this branch."

The old man caught hold of the branch and the dragon let go. The branch snapped back just like a catapult and the old man thought his arms might be ripped out of their sockets. As he followed the branch, the old man decided to let go and he flew through the air like a bird. When he landed, he fell on a poor rabbit and killed it.

The dragon was surprised to see the old man jerked through the air and then fall to the ground. "Was the branch too strong for you, my friend?"

"By no means," replied the old man. "I saw a rabbit over here and decided to catch it, and so I have." He held up the hare for the dragon to see.

The dragon was impressed. He thought to himself, "I'd better be careful. This old man is very clever."

When they got to the dragon's palace, the old man bowed to the dragon's wife and presented her with the hare. She thought it would be wonderful to have a stew that night for supper.

The dragon asked the old man to take a pitcher, go down to the well, and bring back some water for the stew. The old man took one look at the dragon-sized pitcher and knew he couldn't lift it while it was empty, let alone filled with water. He asked the dragon for a shovel.

"Why do you need a shovel to bring back the water?" asked the dragon.

"I'm going to dig around the well and bring the whole thing back to you on my back. Then we won't have to go to the well for several days."

The dragon was shocked. "No, brother, that won't do at all. When the well is dry, we'll all die of thirst."

"I'm sorry, Brother. Its either the whole well or nothing," cried the old man.

"I will fetch the water myself," said the dragon. "Why don't you go into the forest and bring back a nice oak tree for the fire."

The old man walked into the forest and began to make a bark rope. He twined it around and around a grove of trees. The dragon came looking for his guest and found him tying the grove together.

"What are you doing?" the dragon asked.

"I'm not going to waste my time with just one tree, so I decided I'd bring this entire grove to the palace. This way you and your wife will have firewood for weeks."

"No, Brother, please leave my forest as it is."

"All or none," said the old man, so the dragon pulled a tree up by its roots and brought it back to the palace himself.

That evening, the old man, the dragon, and his wife enjoyed their supper, talked a while, and finally said goodnight. After the dragon had gone to bed, the old man crept out of his room and listened at the dragon's door as he and his wife were talking.

"I'm really afraid that this old man will forget his oath and kill us both as we sleep," said the dragon.

"Why don't you take your huge club and hit him on the head while he sleeps? Then you can forget about being afraid."

Hearing this, the old man hurried back to his room where he took a log and carefully dressed it in his nightclothes and pulled the blankets over it. Then, he hid in the closet. The dragon came in and whack, whack, whack, hit the log with his club and went back to sleep.

In the morning, the old man came down to breakfast to the surprise of the dragon and his wife. "Brother, I slept terribly last night," he said. "There was a fly that kept landing on my head."

Once again, the dragon shook with fear. "Shouldn't you be on your way home today?" he said.

"I came out to seek my fortune, and if I return without something to show for my travels, my wife will be upset with me."

The dragon hurriedly went to his treasure room and came back with an enormous sack filled with gold and jewels. "Here, Brother, take this to your wife with my compliments."

The old man knew he could never lift that sack of treasure. "Brother, didn't I bring your wife the rabbit for our supper myself? It would be rude for you not to take this to my wife yourself."

"I would be happy to take it to her," replied the dragon anxiously.

The dragon hoisted the sack onto his back and they walked off to the old man's home. When they got to the clearing, the man asked the dragon to wait there, saying that he must tie up the dogs and prepare his family for the dragon's visit. The dragon waited patiently beside the bag of gold and jewels.

The old man went into his little hovel and gave each of his children a knife and fork and told them what to do. Then, he called to the dragon, "Come on, my friend, the dogs are all tied up."

The dragon slowly crept to the door and just as he was about to open it and walk in, all of the children ran out waving their knives and forks and screaming, "Hurray! Father has brought us a dragon for our supper. Let's kill him and eat him up."

The dragon threw down the sack of treasure and ran for his life, swearing never to come near the old man's home again. When he got to his palace, he barred the door and refused to go outside for a week.

The old man took the dragon's money and bought a fine new house, a farm, and new clothes for his wife and children, and they never were poor again.

I really do feel sorry for the dragon in this story. The old man reminds me of Jack in Jack in the Giant's New Ground—*they must be cousins.*

There is a great version of this tale in The Red King and the Witch *by Ruth Manning-Sanders.*

The Old Woman and the Devil

Palestine

One day an old woman and the devil met near a well and started to talk. Each of them professed to be skilled at sowing sorrow and discontent, and since neither would acknowledge the other as better, they decided to have a contest.

Together they went to the bazaar and stood in front of the butcher's stall as a customer ordered his meat. When the butcher had weighed the purchase the customer refused it, saying, "You have short-weighted me. Don't you know that God commands an honest scale?"

The butcher was outraged. "Are you calling me a cheat and an unbeliever?"

The devil now fanned the flames and goaded them through his wiles to make more accusations, shout louder and louder, get angrier and angrier, insult each other more and more until finally, the butcher grabbed a knife from off his block and stabbed the man killing him there in his stall. The authorities came and took the butcher away.

"See my power, old woman. In one little argument I was able to have one soul killed and another taken to prison. Both lives ruined. Now you see who is the greater at mischief."

"Before we rush to conclusions, just follow me," replied the old woman.

The devil and the old woman walked down a crowded street and came to the shop of a cloth merchant. She went inside and began talking to the merchant.

"I have need of a length of cloth, your finest, my friend. My son, may God forgive him, has a mistress and takes her an expensive present every time he visits her. I know it is terrible and that they are both shameless, but he is my son and I beg God to forgive me. If I do not do what my son asks, he becomes angry with me and yells and beats me. And threatens to drive me from his house and force me to become a beggar on the streets."

"I have a beautiful piece of Aleppo cloth for her. But remember that you may look to God for your reward." She thanked him and paid the price for the cloth, tucking it under her shawl as she walked out into the street.

She then walked straight to the cloth merchant's house and knocked on the door. When his young wife answered, she said, "It is almost time for afternoon prayers and I am so far from my home. May I come in and say my prayers in your home?"

The young woman was happy to help the old woman and let her use her own sitting room. When the old woman was alone, she took the Aleppo cloth and hid it in a basket where clothes were kept. After a while she left the room and, thanking the lady of the house, she walked out into the street.

"Let's see what follows now," she told the devil.

The husband returned from his shop and took off his jacket and placed it on the clothes basket. He saw a piece of cloth sticking out, and, on further examination, he knew that it was the Aleppo cloth that he had sold the old woman for her son's mistress. He was furious. He ran to his wife and accused her of adultery and screamed at her to leave his house and never come back. She pleaded her innocence, but he would not listen and forced her to return to her parents' house in shame and tears.

"So am I your equal?" asked the old woman of the devil.

"Well you did come between a man and his wife and I will concede it was cleverly done, but ..." The devil would not acknowledge the old woman's skills to be as great as his own.

"Now just watch as I prove how great my powers are," said the old woman.

The next day they returned to the shop of the cloth merchant. "I feel so terrible, but I must buy another piece of that cloth that I purchased yesterday. I misplaced it, you see. It was close to prayer time and, since I was far from my own house, I stopped at the home of a young woman. She said I could say my prayers there and I must have set the cloth down and forgotten about it. I left the house after her kindness but cannot remember the name of the street. Do you have more of that cloth?"

The merchant went into the back room and came out with the piece of Aleppo cloth. She took it from him and asked, "This is the same piece. How did you find it?"

"It was my home you stopped by yesterday to say your prayers." He gave her the cloth and closed his shop. He could only think of how unjust he had been to his wife and how he would go to her parents' home and beg her forgiveness. He would never mistrust her again.

The old woman turned to the devil and spoke softly, "You see, not only can I bring discord but I can repair what I have done. I brought peace back to these two. But once you sow your seeds there is no going back."

"I agree," said the devil, "Old women are craftier than the devil himself."

The devil met his match in this story and paid the price by eating a little humble pie. A wonderful version can be found in the book Arab Folktales *by Inea Bushnaq.*

The Thief

Korea

Long ago, there was a thief, not just any thief, but the greatest thief that ever lived. The police knew he was a thief, but could not catch him. The judges knew he was a thief, but could not try him. Even the king himself knew of this thief, but nothing could be done, for he was never caught in the act and never left behind any evidence behind. But, thieves are like any other person—they grow old.

One day, when the thief was an old man, he was shopping for spices in a local shop. When he reached for his wallet, he realized he had left it at home.

He smiled to himself and thought, "What do I need money for? I'm a thief."

He slipped the jar of spice into his sleeve and, waving good bye to the owner of the shop, walked out the door.

As he walked down the street, a hand caught him by the shoulder and spun him around. It was a young police officer.

"I watched you through the shop window and saw you steal that jar of spice," said the young officer.

"Wait," he exclaimed as he recognized the thief, "You are the thief my father always talked about, the greatest thief of all times. My father always wanted to catch you. He will be so proud of me."

And so, the thief was taken to court. "You!" the magistrate roared when he recognized him. "I've always wanted to try you in my court. What did he steal?"

"A jar of spice worth about five copper pennies," said the officer.

"Well, for your sentence, you will pay me five thousand gold pieces."

The old thief was shocked. "I don't have five thousand gold pieces."

The judge smiled. "Then you will spend five thousand days in prison."

"I am an old man," he cried. "Five thousand days could be the rest of my life."

"I hope so," said the magistrate.

The thief was taken to the king's own prison, the strongest in the land. It sat high up on a mountain with walls that rose so high they seemed to meet the sky.

They led him to a cell that was cold and damp, with bars so thick as to almost blot out the sun and an oaken door that creaked as it opened, as if to invite him to a lengthy stay.

"I am going to escape," said the old thief to his guard.

The guard laughed. "No one has ever escaped from the king's prison. If anyone did escape, whichever guard was on duty at the time would have to take the prisoner's place and serve out their sentence. No one ever escapes."

"Watch me," whispered the old man.

When his food was brought to him the next morning, the thief asked if he could be taken to see the king. The thief told his guard that he had a wonderful gift for the king and would like to give it to him personally.

The guard laughed and teased the old man. The old man seemed to speak to himself, muttering, "I wonder what the king will say to this guard when he finds out he kept me from giving him a wondrous gift?" The guard knew the king.

The next morning the thief found himself in the king's throne room. There the king sat, his prime minister next to him, the general of the army next, and finally the bishop of the church. The king looked impatient.

"I haven't much time. Let me have this wonderful gift."

The thief bowed and held out a small golden box, covered with intricate carvings.

The king smiled as he held it but upon opening the box his mood darkened.

"This is a peach pit! A dried, shrunken peach pit."

"Yes, my king, but it is also more, it is a magic peach pit. When you put the pit into the ground in only one day it will grow into a tree. The second day, it will be covered in fruit. By the third day, each piece of fruit will turn to solid gold."

"If that is so, then why haven't you planted it?" asked the king.

"Well, I would if I could, but part of the magic is that you must have a pure heart. You must have never lied, or stolen, or cheated, or hurt someone. I am a thief so the magic won't work for me. But you, you are the king. I'm sure it will work for you."

The king looked down at that peach pit lying in the palm of his hand and thinking of all the times he had lied to his people, all the times he had needlessly hurt them. "No, I'm not the one," he whispered. He handed it back.

" No?" said the thief. "Well, maybe the prime minister, the man who runs the government, can make it grow." He handed it to the prime minister.

The prime minister held that pit and thought of all the bribes he'd taken though the years and all the people who had suffered because of his corruption. "No it's not me," he said sadly.

"Not you?" said the thief. "Well, I'm sure the general, the leader of our armies, can make it grow." He gave the general the peach pit.

The general looked down at that shrunken pit and he thought of all the weeping mothers and widows who had lost their loved ones over a scrap of land or a forgotten idea or misplaced word. "No, I can't do it," he said.

"Really?" said the thief. "I'm sure the bishop, a man of holiness and piety, can make it grow." He handed the pit to the bishop.

The bishop looked down at that peach pit lying in the palm of his hand and remembered all the money that should have gone to the poor and hungry that instead went into his pockets. "No, I'm not the one," he said ruefully and handed it back.

The four men bowed their heads and couldn't even look at the thief.

"Isn't this curious," said the thief accusingly. "The four most powerful men in the kingdom cannot make the magic happen and yet you live lives of wealth and luxury. While I, an old thief, am condemned to spend the rest of my days in prison, for stealing a jar of spice. Does this seem fair?"

There was a moment of silence. Finally, the king spoke, "No thief, it isn't fair. The lesson you taught us today has bought your freedom. Go home."

The thief bowed. As he left the room, he looked at his guard and winked. "I told you I'd escape," he whispered.

I enjoy watching the faces in an audience as they begin to understand what the thief is up to in this tale. This story is found in several Asian cultures, including China. I first read it in Joanna Cole's excellent book Best-Loved Folktales of the World.

The Old Man and the Devil

Siberia

Once upon a time there lived an old man and an old woman. The wife was bad tempered and quarreled with her husband every day. She was always contradicting him and finding fault with his every deed. One day, while the couple were in the forest collecting firewood, they came to a deep chasm in the earth. The old man warned his wife about getting too close, but, ignoring him as she always did and being very curious, she leaned so far over the edge that she fell deep into the earth. The old man called and called, but no answer came from the depths of that crack, so he went home alone.

After only one day, he was lonely. Maybe his life with his wife had been unpleasant, but at least she was some company. He went back to that deep chasm, called loudly to his wife thinking she might hear him, and threw a rope down, hoping to pull her out. Once he felt it hit bottom, he started to pull it up. He pulled and pulled, feeling something heavy on the other end of the rope getting closer and closer. Finally the old man pulled the rope up, out of the chasm, but, instead of his wife at the other end, the old man was facing the devil himself. At first the old man at first was frightened of the devil, but the devil assured the man not to worry. The devil felt nothing but gratitude and planned to reward the old man.

"Yesterday, a bad-tempered old woman came crashing down through the roof of hell and immediately began to make life unbearable for everyone there. You've saved me from her evil ways and I'm going to reward you."

"Reward me? How?"

"We'll work together here on earth. I'll make people sick and I'll teach you how to cure them. Everyone will be so thankful that they'll pay you any amount you ask."

The devil taught the old man how to stroke the brow of a sick person and just mumble a few words that meant nothing at all. That was all that was needed. The devil would leave the sick room and they would be cured immediately.

And so the old man went into partnership with the devil. Soon he was a wealthy man, respected and loved by all for his magic cures.

One day, the devil approached the old man and told him that the Tsar's daughter was ill and she would soon die. Nothing could save her and the old man should stay away from her sick room.

Indeed, the Tsar's daughter was dying. Knowing of his reputation as a healer, the Tsar sent for the old man, but the old man refused to visit the dying princess. The Tsar offered him mountains of gold and valleys of silver, but the old man refused to visit the sick girl. The ruler offered him ships filled with jewels and wagons loaded down with silks and furs, but still the old healer refused to come to the palace. Finally, the Tsar ordered him to save his daughter or suffer the pain of torture and death. That was an offer the old man could not refuse, so he slowly made his way to the palace. As soon as he entered the palace, he was taken to the dying girl's room, where the devil sat, crouched beside the bed, invisible to all but the old man.

"What are you doing here?" hissed the devil. "I told you not to come and cure her."

The old man looked innocent and said, "I only came to tell you that the old woman has crawled out of the chasm and is looking everywhere for you. In fact, she stands right outside the palace door as we speak."

The devil shrieked in terror and disappeared in a wisp of smoke. The Tsar's daughter was instantly cured and the old man was richly rewarded.

He took his wealth and moved far away to a country where no one knew him or his reputation as a healer. There he lived happily for many more years.

Stories about tricking the devil or any evil spirit are as old as the human race and found in every corner of the world. This one has a particularly satisfying ending. A version can be found in The Fairy Tale Tree *by Vladislav Stanovsky and Jan Vladislav.*

The Mocker Mocked

Armenia

Once, a long time ago, there was a king who lived in a country far away to the East. This king had a habit of sitting on his balcony at the end of the day, when all his work of state was done. He would watch his subjects as they passed by, listening to them talk about their day, and their problems, and the way they felt about this and that. In this way, the King knew what his people thought about the issues of the time and about their ruler.

One day, the king was sitting on his balcony when he saw the most unusual of sights. Scurrying along the road was a little old woman. She was misshapen and bent over; her face was twisted and covered in warts; and it seemed she had a permanent sneer. The king could not believe his eyes.

"I have never seen anything so hideous," he called out for all to hear. "That old crone is by far the most repulsive creature I have ever seen. Is it a cave or a hollow log that she calls home?" The king laughed and laughed so hard that the old woman could not help but hear him, but she walked on, paying him no heed.

The king began to notice her more and more, and each time he saw her, his taunts and mocking became more and more intolerable. One day, after the king had laughed and jeered more than usual, the old woman stopped.

She looked up at the king and slowly, deliberately spoke to him. "Laugh if you will, laugh if you must, but mark my words, I will have the last laugh." With that, she walked away.

Now, the king didn't know it and neither do you, but, I'll tell you that this old crone was a witch and one of her special powers was the ability to change her form into anything she wanted. She took thousands of shapes, some as beautiful as the shape seen by the king was ugly.

The king didn't stop his mocking of the old woman, and one day, he went too far. The witch decided to seek her revenge. The next morning, she changed her shape into that of a lovely young woman and she went to see the queen.

When she was in the queen's chambers, fell to her knees and spoke. "Oh, my queen, I am just a poor young widow and I need to provide for my young children. Please take me into your service. I will work hard each day to please you and to feed and clothe my children."

Now, the queen was a beautiful woman, both in her face and in her soul. When she heard the story of the young widow, she was moved. She told the young woman that she could work as a maid and that she should return the next day to help the queen at her bath.

The next day, the old witch, still disguised, accompanied the queen to the bathhouse. As the witch began to comb the queen's long hair, a change took place. The queen, herself, began to change into a grotesque beast. Her hair became matted and smelly, her breath turned foul, and her body was quickly covered in coarse hair and running sores.

When the queen looked into a mirror, she screamed, "My husband, my husband, come quickly!"

At her words, the witch vanished.

The king was horrified. His beautiful wife was more hideous than any creature he had ever seen.

"What has happened?" he cried.

The queen told him of the young woman who had asked for work. "As the comb she was holding passed through my hair, I was changed. Find her, make her change me back. Please, I beg you."

The king didn't know which way to turn, where to look or who to ask for help. Soldiers were sent to look through the city, but there were so many young women. How would they ever find her?

The old crone, however, was back in her home. She was beginning to feel guilty about what she had done. The queen was a good woman and should not suffer just because her husband was thoughtless. She walked to the palace and asked to be admitted. The guards, when they saw the old creature, would not let her enter.

"Away with you, old hag. Find someone else to bother. Our king has enough on his mind."

The king heard the commotion and called out his window, ordering the guards to bring the old woman to him. When they were alone in the throne room, she spoke.

"Your majesty, I am the old woman you always laugh at from your balcony, and I am the young woman who changed your queen. How does it feel to be mocked? Are you still laughing?"

"Old woman," said the king, "give me back my queen and I will give you your weight in gold. I will give you a fine palace. I will give you power and position." The king pleaded.

The witch laughed.

"Why do you laugh, old woman?"

"Because, it's my turn."

"Bring your wife to me and I will change her back, not for your sake, but for hers. Next time you see someone whose appearance or manner is different than yours, perhaps you will treat them kindly."

The queen came into the room and the old witch touched her hair. The queen returned to her former shape and was beautiful once again. The old woman vanished.

From that day on the king was a different man. It seemed as if he looked at people in a different light, no matter their differences, no matter their faults, treating each person with fairness and respect. So may we all learn that lesson.

I first heard this story from my grandmother, but she never taught it to me. I often wonder why she taught me some stories but not others. You can find a version in Armenian Folk-tales and Fables *by Charles Downing, Oxford University Press.*

The Traveler and the Four Young Men

Burma (Myanmar)

Once there were four young men who passed their time creating the most far-fetched and incredible tales. One day they saw an old man who was traveling from one city to another and had stopped in their village for rest and a meal. The old man's clothes were quite expensive and, on seeing them, the young men soon were filled with envy. They decided to hatch a plan that would enable them to take the old man's clothes for their own. Soon they came up with a wonderful idea. They would challenge him to a contest. Each one would tell an improbable adventure and, if any man doubted the truth of any story, that man would become the slave of the storyteller.

When he heard their proposal, the traveler agreed. He finished his meal and settled down to listen to each young man as he took his turn weaving his elaborate lie. In fact, everyone in the shop stopped and listened and wondered who would win this contest.

The first young man began. "Before I was even born my mother asked my father to pick her some plums from the tree in front of their house. My father replied that the tree was too high and too dangerous to climb. My mother asked the same favor of my brothers and sisters and they gave her the same answer. I was so upset that my mother was disappointed and hungry for those plums that I climbed the tree myself and picked the plums when no one was looking. I left them on the table near where my mother rested. No one knew where the plums came from, but my mother was pleased."

The four young men watched the old traveler to see if he would protest and express his disbelief, but he merely nodded his head quietly as if the story were commonplace.

The second young man began. "When I was only a week old I took a walk through the forest. As I walked I grew hungry and found a date tree. I climbed up into the date tree and ate and ate until I was so full and sleepy that I could not climb down. So I went back to the village and borrowed a ladder, which I carried to the tree, propped against its trunk, and climbed down. If I hadn't used that ladder I would still be up in that date tree."

They all looked at the old man, but again he merely nodded in agreement.

The third young man began. "When I was one year old I was walking in the tall grasses at the edge of the village when I saw a rabbit. I chased the creature until I caught it, only to discover that it was not a rabbit at all, but a tiger—a very hungry tiger. The beast roared and opened its mouth to eat me. I tried to explain that I thought he was a rabbit and would never chase a tiger, but this only enraged him further. He opened his great jaws to bite me, but I caught hold of him and broke him in two and went on my way, still looking for a rabbit."

The old man nodded his head in agreement.

The fourth and last young man began his story. "Last year I went fishing on a nearby lake. I fished all morning, but caught nothing. I asked others who were there fishing but none of them had caught anything either. I decided to find the cause of this problem and dove off the side of the boat and into the water. I swam down for about three days until I reached the bottom. There I found a huge fish as big as a mountain, eating every fish that passed by its enormous mouth. I killed the monster with one blow from my fist. Then I realized I was hungry, so I lit a fire and roasted the huge beast and ate the whole thing. After a nap I floated to the surface and went home."

Again the traveler only nodded his head in agreement.

Now it was the old man's turn. "On my farm I have a fruit tree that is different from any other tree in the world. It has no leaves but it does have four branches. Years ago, at the end of each branch, a single fruit grew. When the fruit was ripe I picked it and, when I cut each piece open a young man jumped out. As they came from my tree on my property, these men were legally mine. I made them work on my farm, but they were very lazy. The only thing they wanted to do all day was sit around and make up fantastic stories. After a few weeks, all four men ran away and since that time I have been traveling all over the countryside looking for them. Now, here in this shop, I have found them at last. You know well enough that you are my runaway servants. Now, come back with me and don't give me any more trouble."

The four young tricksters couldn't say a word. They were in a hopeless position. If they declared his story to be true they were admitting to being his runaway servants. If they said the story was false they would lose the contest and become his slaves anyway. They hung their heads in silence.

The villagers who were watching smiled at their dilemma. Finally, the head of the village declared the traveler to be the winner. The old man turned to the four young scoundrels and said, "Now you are my slaves and everything you own belongs to me, so take off your clothes, and shoes, and rings, and give them to me and I will give you your freedom." The four young men agreed.

The old traveler tied their belongings into a bundle, threw them over his shoulder and resumed his journey, leaving the four young men standing naked and bewildered in the village shop. You can rest assured the story was told over and over again, always at their expense.

The tradition of lying for a wager can be found in many cultures—the story "Lying for a Wager" is an Eastern European tale I heard as a boy. This one from Burma has a great twist at the end. You can find a version in Ride with the Sun *by Harold Courlander.*

Chapter Three

Heroes

Beowulf and the Dragon

England

Battles raged and swords were drawn, and Hygelac, the king of the Geats, was slain. Beowulf, then, became king and ruled well for fifty winters, while his hair turned silver and the lines on his face became like a map of his land.

One day, a great shadow passed over the land. A fierce dragon, his wings blocking the sun, burned villages and killed the people of Geatland by the score. Centuries before this, a warrior king, the last of his people, had stored all their wealth in a barrow, deep in the side of a cliff, its passageway cleverly hidden. The warrior placed all the gold, jewels, and silver of his clan into that barrow and then wrought a powerful curse that was meant to keep the hoard safe until the last day in time. For hundreds of years the curse held and the barrow was undisturbed. Then, the dragon came searching among the rocks for a hiding place, found the barrow, and made it his lonely den. He gathered the treasure around his bed, counting his new wealth and gloating over his find.

For three hundred years the dragon lived contentedly. Then, once again, the treasure was disturbed. A slave, having displeased the man who owned him, fled in fear. Looking for a place to hide and avoid the wrath of his master, the man searched among the cliffs and rocks for a hiding place. There, he stumbled upon the secret path that led to the dragon's lair. As the morning light reached its fingers into the ancient cave, the slave saw the mounds of gold and jewels scattered around the dragon's sleeping body. When he saw the fire serpent, the man was terrified, but the treasure that surrounded the creature quenched the poor man's fear long enough for him to snatch a golden goblet that lay not far from the monster's head. Silently, the slave made his way out of the cave, and then, to his master, where he offered up the golden vessel and begged forgiveness.

When the dragon woke, he counted his hoard as he did every day and found that the golden goblet was missing. He slithered throughout the barrow, counting and recounting, looking and then looking some more. Finally he came upon the scent of the man. His anger turned to rage and his rage turned to all-consuming thoughts of revenge. He would punish every one of the Geats for the sin of this one man. So, the fire serpent took to the air and attacked the surrounding villages and farms, burning buildings, animals and people, alike. Terror spread throughout the land and fear settled into the hearts of the Geats.

As the day turned to night, the dragon crept back to its lair, certain that he had terrified the Geats and that he was secure in his hidden stronghold. But, for all of his cunning, the Dragon had forgotten something very important—Beowulf was king of the Geats and Beowulf protected his people.

When word of the fire serpent's raids reached Beowulf, he rose in anger. He saw that his great hall had been reduced to ashes and heard that warriors, women, and children had been terrified and killed by the beast. Gathering his men, he announced that he would kill the fiend.

Beowulf's ring warriors begged and pleaded with him to let the monster lie in its lair and rot there till the end of the world, but the great king would hear none of their words.

"I am no longer a young man," Beowulf told them, "but I will always be the shield of my people. I have no fear of this serpent and am not intimidated by his great strength and cunning. I killed Grendel and his mother. I have fought and slain many sea serpents. I have fought in battles too numerous to number and have always won. I shall go to this dragon without an army, accompanied by only a dozen of my finest warriors, and I shall meet this beast alone at his lair."

The old king went to his armorer and had him fashion a shield of shining iron. He knew that his wooden shields would be of little protection against the fire serpent. Then the great lord of the rings learned what had caused the dragon's anger and ordered the thief to lead him and twelve of his bravest warriors to the serpent's barrow.

When they arrived at a place not far from the dragon's lair, Beowulf told his men to wait for him there. "This is my fight and mine alone," he said. "With my shield and my great sword, Naegling, I will fight and kill the serpent. I will win his hoard of gold and avenge my people or, if Wyrd, the ruler of all, is not with me this day, I will die."

As Beowulf neared the mouth of the cave he called out to the dragon, challenging him to come out and fight in the open. Then, Beowulf raised his iron shield, drew the mighty Naegling and waited.

The dragon roared his defiance and rushed out to meet the king. Beowulf raised his trusted sword and struck the monster, but the blade that had saved his life so many times was now blunted by the thick hide of the dragon. And his shield of iron grew red hot under the fire of the dragon's breath. In that moment, the old hero knew the gods might not protect him this day as they had done so many times in the past. Still, knowing that this could be his last battle, the great king of the Geats did not want to die without taking his enemy with him. He raised his sword and struck again and again at the dragon, but it was of no use.

Each blow seemed to enrage the monster more and more until the serpent spat out a cloak of fire that engulfed the king.

The warriors who had accompanied Beowulf rushed forward, but seeing this, they lost heart and ran for the woods to save themselves. Everyone, that is, except the youngest, Wiglaf, nephew to the king. He turned to his comrades and cried out, "We were chosen by our king as the bravest warriors, the ones he wanted at his side. How can we desert the lord who gave us the war rings we wear on our arms? Show your bravery. Fight at his side."

But the warriors still hid in fear. So Wiglaf turned and shouted at them once again. "I, for one, will not live the life of a coward. I would rather die at the side of my king, giving him the last of my courage."

With these words, Wiglaf ran to Beowulf. "My king, do you remember the deeds of your youth when no foe could vanquish you in battle? Summon all your skill and strength and fight for your life. I am at your side."

Seeing Wiglaf, the dragon attacked again. Wiglaf's shield could not protect him and he took shelter with Beowulf behind the shield of iron. With his nephew at his side, Beowulf again attacked the serpent and drove his sword Naegling deep into the dragon's head. But Naegling, that sword that had conquered so many, betrayed the king in his last battle. As his sword broke, Beowulf fell back. The dragon, seeing this retreat, lunged and sank his teeth into the king. Beowulf could feel his own life's blood rush from his body.

Wiglaf, seeing his king fall, ran at the dragon and charged through a wall of flame to drive his sword deep into the serpent's chest. The great creature began to stagger and his fire began to diminish. Despite his grievous wounds, Beowulf rose and stabbed at the beast over and over again with his dagger until it was almost torn in two and fell dead at the old warrior's feet. This was his last triumph. Beowulf fell back against the cave wall, his wounds burning and the dragon's poison surging through his veins.

Turning to Wiglaf, he said, "The fire serpent lies dead. Go quickly to its lair and bring out some of the treasure that I have won for my people. Let me see it so that it will be easier for me to die—to give up the kingdom I love so much and end my time as king of the Geats."

Inside the cave, Wiglaf saw wonders of gold and jewels. He filled his cloak with cups and platters and took the golden banner down to deliver it to Beowulf. The king admired the treasure and then spoke again to Wiglaf. "Look after my people. When they have burned my body, have a barrow built on Whale's Ness to serve as a beacon for those who travel the seas. Call it Beowulf's Barrow to remind my people of my deeds and my love for them."

Then Beowulf took off his gold collar ring, his golden helmet, and the battle shirt that had saved him so many times and gave them to Wiglaf. "You are the last of my kinsmen. Wyrd has taken all the rest before me and now it is my turn to follow them." With these words Beowulf, the king of Geats, the hero of his people and the lord of the rings, died. His spirit rose to meet his kin and savor the rewards of a legend.

Wiglaf banished the cowards that had abandoned their king. Then, he called together those who remained of the shield band, those warriors upon whom Beowulf had bestowed rings of glory. Beowulf was taken to Whale's Ness and prepared for his burning.

"Let our king take the treasure he has won with him," said Wiglaf. "No Geat will wear these treasures or enjoy their beauty. A treasure that brings such sorrow can give gladness to no one. Without Beowulf we will hear the raven's cry above the bodies of our dead warriors, we will face our enemies without our shield, our people will know only dark days without their shepherd."

The treasure was heaped at Beowulf's feet and followed him into the next life. A great burial mound was built and his ashes were buried deep inside, with the treasure that did not burn. The twelve bravest warriors rode around and around the barrow singing the deeds of Beowulf for all to hear. The burial mound became a beacon to those who sailed the sea, as Beowulf had been a beacon to his people.

I love the Beowulf story but always wondered why most storytellers ended the story with the death of Grendel's mother. The story of Beowulf as an old hero, still able to slay the dragon to protect his people, is so rich in its beauty and sorrow. There are so many versions of Beowulf to choose from, but I do like the one by the poet Seamus Heaney the best.

The Doll That Caught a Thief

United States

It happened a long time ago that all the folks who were staying at a certain tavern were robbed. Now in those days the taverns were places where travelers could spend the night, resting up before they continued their journeys. On this particular night, all the doors and windows of the establishment were locked and bolted and in the morning no one was missing from among the guests. The owner, who was an honest man, decided that all the folks who had spent the night should stay and together, they would try to sort the problem out.

"The reputation of my house is on the line here," he said. "We have to recover those valuables or folks won't want to stay the night under my roof."

It turned out that everyone had lost money, so much money that the sum they calculated was about three thousand gold pieces. Several gold watches and a snuffbox were missing, too. "That snuffbox has been in my family for generations," said the owner. "I would not part with it for one hundred dollars."

Everyone searched the house, but nothing could be found. Finally an old woman among the travelers spoke up, "My doll can find the thief." Everyone turned and gave her a strange look—a look of disbelief.

"Its true," she said, walking into a room at the back of the tavern where she pulled a little wooden doll from her bag and set it on the table. Then she took some walnut juice and spread it all over the doll. When she came out of the room she turned to the owner and said, "Have those travelers go in there one by one. Each person must go in alone and grab the doll and swear that he or she did not steal anything last night. The doll will stay quiet when touched by an honest person, but will scream and holler when the thief grabs hold of it." The guests all thought this was foolishness, but at this point they would agree to try anything. One by one, each person went into the back room with the doll and then came back out again.

When they were all through, the old woman asked if everyone had taken hold of the doll. They all insisted they had, so she asked them to line up and hold their hands out with their palms up. She looked at each ones' hands and then pointed at the man who had claimed his snuffbox was stolen. "He is the thief," she said. At first he denied it, but when a rope was produced the man spoke up loudly.

"If you hang me you'll never find your money. I hid it where no one could find it, but if you promise to let me go I'll tell you where it is hidden."

Well, the owner of the tavern wanted to hang him then and there, but the other folks wanted their valuables back. They promised to release him and took an oath on the bible. He told them to look in a hollow log at the bottom of the woodpile near the old cook stove. When the money was found, the thief was freed and given a head start. It wasn't really necessary for him to run since no one was bothering to chase him anyway.

The travelers decided to have a celebration at the thief's expense by raffling off his watch. The man who won the watch turned and gave it to the old woman. A hat was passed and many a silver or gold coin found its way into that hat. The tavern owner turned to the woman and said, "All this money is yours if you can tell us how you caught that thief."

"Well, didn't you hear my doll scream and holler?" she asked. Everyone said no, they didn't.

She smiled and said, "You folks are all honest, so you went into the room and grabbed hold of that doll. But a thief is suspicious and he probably knew there was a trick to it all, so he never touched the doll. All I did was look for the one person whose hands were not stained with walnut juice."

The owner handed her the hat full of money and thanked her for saving his good name. The old woman smiled and put her doll back in her bags.

This riddle story is found throughout the United States, especially in the southern mountains. There are also many variations found in other cultures. Obviously thieves throughout the world should spend more time listening to stories! Suzanne Barchers has a version of this story in her book Wise Women.

The Story Bag

Korea

Once a long time ago there was a rich family who had one son, and this boy loved to have stories told to him. Whenever he met a new person he would ask for a story. Every time he heard a story he would carefully place it in a small bag he always carried at his side. He heard so many stories and put so many in that bag that soon it was stuffed and he had to push and push to get another one in the bag. He was so worried that one might escape that he tied the bag shut with a strong cord.

The boy grew to be a handsome young man and the time came for him to take a bride. The families arranged the marriage and soon his parent's house was in a joyous uproar as preparations were made to welcome the bride to her new home.

There was an old servant in this house that had known the young man since he was a small child. The old man had told the boy stories and had taught him to fish and name the birds that came to perch in the trees that filled the garden. He had watched him grow to be a fine young man. The servant was working alone in the kitchen, remembering the old days of the boy's youth, when he thought he heard whispering coming from somewhere nearby. He listened carefully and realized that the voices were coming from a bag that hung on a hook in a small storage closet. It was the bag that held the boy's stories. As the voices spoke, the old man listened.

"Listen to me. The boy is to be wed tomorrow. For too many years he has kept us in this bag, so crowded we can barely remember who we are or how we are told. He has tortured us and now it is time for revenge."

"I have an idea," cried one voice. "He will take his horse and ride to bring his bride home. I will change myself into tempting red berries growing by the roadside and he will stop to taste me, but I will be poisonous and he will die in agony." All the voices laughed.

A second voice spoke up, "If that does not work I will become a bubbling brook by the side of the road and when he sees me he will grow thirsty and drink deeply of my poisonous waters."

A third voice almost screamed in glee, "If that fails, I will become an iron skewer, heated until red hot, and I will hide in the ceremonial bag of chaff that is prepared for him at his bride's home. When he arrives on his horse and steps down onto the bag I will burn his feet and he will cry out in agony."

"If all this fails," cried another, "I will become poisonous string snakes, thin as threads and deadly in their bite. I will hide beneath the bed in their bridal chamber and when they have fallen asleep I will kill them both."

The stories laughed as if they were mad and perhaps they had gone mad during all those years of being tied up in a bag. The old servant heard their plans and feared for his young master's safety. He knew that the only way to stop the vengeance of the stories was to accompany the young man in his journey to bring his bride home.

The next day the young man was ready to set out when the old servant came running from the house and took hold of the bridle reins. "I have known this young man all his life" said the old man, "and I want to lead him to his bride."

The master of the house tried to persuade the old servant to remain behind, but the man was determined to make the journey. And so he set off, leading the young man's horse down the road. As they walked along, the two men came to a field that was full of bright red berries. Suddenly the bridegroom was so hungry that he felt a pain in his belly.

"Stop here and pick me some of those berries."

The old man turned and smiled at him. "Those berries? There are far better ones ahead. Let's wait until later and I'll pick you some that are twice as tasty." As soon as he had ridden past the enticing berries the young man was no longer hungry.

Later they came to a bubbling spring. It was as if the water was singing, telling the young man of its cool refreshing taste.

"Stop and bring me some of that water. I have never been so thirsty in all my life."

Again the old servant just prodded the horse to move faster. "That spring is very salty. Further on there is a spring that tastes almost like wine." As soon as they passed the spring the young man's thirst left him.

In the afternoon they reached the bride's house and the whole family was there to greet the young man as he rode into their courtyard. The servant led the horse to the waiting bag of chaff, but when the bridegroom started to dismount, the old man caused the horse to step forward. Not noticing this, the young man missed the bag, stumbled, and fell to the ground. As he rose, he glared at the servant for making him look like a fool, but he decided not to scold him in front of everyone, knowing it might spoil the wedding.

After the wedding ceremony was performed, the young couple left for the young man's home. When they arrived their marriage was celebrated again, with food and song and toast after toast to the young couple's health and happiness. Finally, the young man and his bride went to their bridal chamber and closed the door. Outside, standing on the veranda and armed with a sword, the faithful servant waited. As soon as the lights were out and the couple stopped talking, the old man rushed into the dark room.

In shock, the young man called out, "Who's there and what do you want?"

"Young master," cried the servant, "There is no time to explain, just take your bride and run as fast as you can from this room."

As the couple leapt from the bed, the servant kicked the bedding away, disturbing hundreds of string snakes that writhed and hissed trying to get at the young couple. But the old man wielded his sword like a true warrior, slashing and stabbing as he whirled and jumped amid the tangle of snakes. Never leaving the room, the young bride and bridegroom watched in horror and then in admiration as the faithful servant killed every snake.

When all was over, the old man turned to his young master and told him all that had happened. He told him of the stories in the bag and their madness, and the many ways they had plotted revenge for the years they had been confined and silenced. When he had heard it all, the young mad went straight to the kitchen and opened the closet that held the bag. Lifting it up, he begged the forgiveness of the stories. As he held the bag it seemed as if their madness had begun to fade. The next day, he sent one of his father's young grooms out into the countryside, riding with the bag to spread the stories to anyone who would listen.

And so it is that stories are to be shared, passed from one person to another over great distances through all time. As long as they are shared and spoken, they are truly alive and well.

This is a well-known folktale about stories. It reminds us that we have a responsibility not only to keep them alive but also to keep them healthy. Found in many collections including Korean Children's Favorite Stories.

The Hunted Soul

England

A long time ago there lived an old Goodwife who would go down to the market in Crowcombe to sell a few of these and a bit of those. She was a stout old woman, and so she and her aged pony Smart took a great deal of time to get to the market. She and Smart had to leave her cottage around four in the morning to get to the market on time. Well, one time the dear old thing rose in the middle of the night and mistook the time. She loaded up old Smart with large baskets filled with eggs and apples and got herself into the saddle and rode off to market just before midnight. She took out her knitting needles and some yarn and started to knit some stockings as she rode along.

Now, old Smart knew the way to the market and after all these years he just pointed his nose toward town and began his slow walk there, but the old Goodwife, she grew sleepy and soon was fast asleep in the saddle, nodding to the slow gait of the walking pony. When she woke she was aware that her pony was standing still. Smart had come to a stop and was shivering, his ears down and his eyes wide with fear. As the old woman looked around she heard the sound of hounds howling in the dark and she saw a little white hare running toward her, terrified. Well, the old Goodwife saw that little hare and was so moved with pity for it that, quick as a thought, she reached down, picked up the little hare, slipped it into one of her baskets, and closed the lid. She tried to get old Smart to start moving again but the old pony would have none of it and just stood there rooted to the ground. She heard the hounds getting closer and closer and decided to start her knitting again as if she had nothing in all the world better to do with her time. As the hounds got closer she could hear the clatter of hooves and soon the hounds and a great black horse came into view as they approached her and Smart. The horse came along side her pony and old Smart's knees went to shaking so hard the old granny thought he might fall down. The rider was wrapped all in a black cloak, a great broad brimmed black hat on his head. The black horse had horns that grew from its head and an eerie green light surrounded the rider and horse and seemed to come out of the mouths of the hounds with each breath.

"Have you seen a rabbit go by?" asked the rider.

Granny knew better than to speak to the rider so she just shook her head no. That was the truth in a way, since the hare had not gone past her but straight into her pannier basket.

The rider stared at her with eyes that blazed and then turned his horse and rode off, leading his hounds toward Will's Neck. Soon the barking of the hounds faded in the night and stillness came to the darkness once again. Then old Smart did something he had not done in twenty years. He lumbered up to a canter and didn't stop until he came to Roebuck Ford. There he stopped, right in the middle of the running water where no harm can come to you from the creatures that hunt from the beyond. When the old Goodwife opened her basket out stepped a beautiful lady.

"How can I ever thank you enough?" she said to the old woman. "When I was young I was a witch and when I died I was condemned to be hunted by the Devil and his pack of hounds each night until the end of time unless I could somehow get behind them. Tonight you put me behind the hunter's pack and saved me." With that she smiled at the old woman, lit up like sunlight on a summer morn, and was gone.

Well, granny and old Smart finished their journey only to find that the old clock on the church at Butter Cross was striking three, so they sat themselves down and finished their night's rest. They had no fear of the hounds ever bothering them again, for the hounds of hell are always wary of anyone—man, woman, or beast—who bests them.

I heard this story one night at the Festival at the Edge in Much Wenlock, Shropshire, England. The teller had joined many others who sit around the campfire to swap tales all night. It's a great story of heroism in spite of fear. You can find a version in Folk Tales of the British Isles *by Michael Foss.*

Rose Red

China

When the Tang dynasty ruled the Middle Kingdom, the sword ruled the world. The first and foremost sword warriors were the sword saints who could change their shape at will. The strokes of their blades were like flashes of lightening across the sky. The men who opposed these sword saints were often dead before they knew they had been cut. But these great swordsmen valued their solitude and did not interfere in the quarrels of men. The swordsmen of the lowest order were merely hired killers, men who were paid to do away with someone's enemies. Death was an everyday matter to them. Not as high as the sword saints and never as low as hired killers, were the sword heroes—men who slew the unjust and defended the oppressed and downtrodden. These swordsmen could fly over rooftops and walk up and down walls. They came without a sound and went without a trace. Molo was a sword hero.

In those days there lived a young man named Tsui, whose father was an official in high standing and a friend of the prince. One day the prince took ill and Tsui was sent by his father to visit the prince and lift his spirits. When he arrived at the palace, Tsui was greeted by three beautiful slave girls, who offered him food and drink. After he had visited the prince he was escorted to the gate by one of the slave girls. Her name was Rose Red. As they walked through the palace grounds Tsui could not take his eyes off the beautiful young woman. Finally, she smiled at him and started to make signs with her hands. First she stretched out three fingers, then she turned her hand around three times, and finally she pointed one finger to a small mirror she wore on a chain around her neck. When they parted at the gate she whispered to him, "Do not forget me."

When Tsui returned home he felt confused by the meeting and the young woman's odd behavior. Now, it happened that the young man, Tsui, had taken into his service an old man named Molo. Unbeknownst to Tsui, Molo was an extraordinary person.

"What troubles you, young master?" asked Molo.

Tsui told Molo all about his chance meeting with the beautiful young woman and the strange hands signals she had shown him.

Molo smiled and said, "I know what she meant, young master. When she stretched out three fingers she was telling you that she is quartered in the third court of the palace. When she turned her hand around three times it meant the sum of three times five fingers, or fifteen. When she pointed to the small mirror she meant that on the fifteenth day, when the moon is as round as the mirror, you are to go for her."

The young man was overjoyed at Molo's words but he turned to the old man and said, "The prince's palace is like no other fortress in the world. The walls are high and a dog that is as ferocious as a tiger guards the door to the women's slave quarters. It would be impossible to enter."

"Nothing is impossible, young master. We will wrap ourselves in dark silk and fly over the walls and across the rooftops. I will take care of the dog when we reach the palace."

Tsui looked at the old man and asked, "Who are you, Molo?"

Molo smiled and said, "I am your humble servant."

On the appointed day they prepared themselves for their adventure. Molo gave Tsui dark silk to wrap around himself like a cloak. He clung to the old man's back and, in one leap, they were over the walls of the palace, flying from roof to roof. Tsui thought he had entered a dream as Molo seemed to glide effortlessly through the air. He left Tsui on the roof of the women's slave quarters and told him to wait.

Molo glided to the ground without a sound and approached the door. The huge dog was waiting, his ears straining to hear every sound, his eyes darting from place to place, looking for any enemy. Molo approached the dog, appearing like a cloud of smoke. The dog sensed something and charged the hazy form, but Molo's sword danced as the dog passed and the animal died in an instant.

Molo returned for Tsui and they dropped to the ground and walked into the slave quarters. Everyone was asleep except Rose Red, who was waiting by the door to the sleeping room.

She took Tsui's hand and almost wept. "I knew you would understand my signs and come for me, but I was so worried about the challenges that you would have to face in this palace. How did you survive?"

Tsui told her about Molo and his powers and how he had understood her signs and brought him to her.

Red Rose fell to her knees and thanked the old man. "Please know that I was not born a slave but am the child of a good family. I will love your master forever if you save me from this place."

The old man smiled and told the young couple to follow him into the courtyard. Red Rose brought what little possessions she had and the two of them held onto Molo's cloak as he rose into the air and began to fly from roof to roof.

They flew over the high walls and past the guards who saw nothing. Down, through the valley below, they flew, and across the broad river to the forest where Tsui's father had a summer home.

When the prince discovered that a slave was missing and that his famous dog lay dead, he knew that only a sword hero could have entered the slave quarters that night. The prince was a proud man and would never want others to know he was vulnerable, so he ordered his guards and advisers to keep the abduction of his slave a secret. But he sent spies out into the countryside to search for Rose Red.

Time passed and after two years the young couple decided that it was safe enough to relax their guard a bit. One day, when Molo was away on an errand, Rose Red went walking near the village that lay on the edge of the forest. The prince's men saw her and followed her home. They reported this to the prince who summoned Tsui to his palace.

"How did you steal my slave?" asked the prince.

Tsui was so frightened of the prince and his power that he told him the whole story. The prince listened in silence and then spoke.

"It was Rose Red that started this whole affair, but now that she is your wife I will not punish either of you. However, to have a man of Molo's power in my kingdom is not acceptable. Molo will have to suffer for his crimes."

The prince ordered a hundred archers to surround the home of Tsui and Rose Red. Their orders were to take Molo captive and bring him to the prince. Seeing the soldiers, Molo flew to the top of the wall that surrounded the house. The arrows were as thick as rain but his sword danced among the flying shafts, shattering them so fast that not one touched him. Molo looked around like a hawk and in an instant he disappeared.

Many years later, one of Tsui's former servants saw Molo in the south of China, selling herbal medicine. The swordsman had not aged a day, and when he saw the man, he smiled and vanished in a cloud of smoke.

I love stories where the hero is an elder and they are not just a wise hero but an actual physical hero as well. This story can be found in The Chinese Fairy Book, *edited by R. Wilhelm and translated by Frederick Martins—sadly long out of print but worth the search for a copy.*

The Wise Woman

Algeria

Long ago, the people of a town were under siege by a cruel invader. The people suffered daily, not only from the weapons of their enemy but also from lack of food, water, and supplies. Many had died and there were few animals left in the town that had not been slaughtered to feed the starving people.

The lord of the city called the town council and other leaders together and announced that it would be futile to hold out any longer. They should throw themselves on the mercy of their enemy and hope that he would find pity for the people who had suffered so much.

Most of those listening knew that his words were true and were resigned to surrendering and begging for mercy. Then an ancient woman by the name of Aicha came forward and spoke.

"I do not feel that we can trust our enemy. I think that if you will all help me we can find a way to defeat them and save our town and our freedom."

The people were willing to grasp any straw of hope. "What do you need?" they asked.

"First, I will need a calf," she said quietly.

The people all declared that a calf had not been seen in the city in weeks. How could they find one?

Aicha insisted and so they searched the town and finally found a calf hidden in the barn of an old miser. They brought it to Aicha.

"Well done, my friends. Now, I need a sack full of corn."

Again, they all declared that not a kernel of corn was to be found in the city, but again Aicha insisted, so they searched. Soon each brought a handful and a pocketful and a cup full until they filled a sack. Aicha took the corn and mixed it with water and fed it to the calf.

The lord protested, "How can you feed a calf when our children are dying of hunger in the streets?"

But Aicha merely said, "Trust me and all will be saved."

When the calf had finished eating she led it to the city gate and told the soldiers to open the gate. When the gates were opened Aicha gently pushed the calf outside and told the soldiers to bar the gates once again. The calf began to graze on the grass between the city and the enemy encampment.

The enemy soldiers quickly seized the calf and brought it to their leader. The king was stunned when he saw the calf.

"What is this all about? I thought that this city was on the verge of starvation but they let a calf out to graze? Well, we will have their calf for our dinner."

When the king's soldiers had slaughtered the calf they found its stomach filled with undigested corn. They immediately told their king.

"If they are feeding their cattle corn then they have more supplies than we do! We can never outlast them in a siege." The king ordered his army to break camp and leave the town immediately.

The next morning the soldiers on the wall of the town saw that the enemy had retreated and abandoned their camp. There was a great celebration and the lord of the city praised Aicha for her wisdom. Aicha basked in the praise of her town's people and lived the rest of her days in honor and comfort.

———————————

Its amazing how wise one becomes when one is wise and daring enough to apply it to a dangerous situation! This is a great story about the wisdom of Aicha, but also about the courage of her people for recognizing and trusting her. A version of this story can be found in the book Wise Women *by Suzanne Barchers.*

The Witch of Kamalalaya

India

The village of Kamalalaya lies at the foot of the Himalayas, a place of beauty and serenity. Or so it seems. In the summer the nearby lake is filled with pink and white lotus blossoms. It is from this lake and its flowers that the village took its name Kamalalaya, which means the home of the lotus.

In this village, many years ago, there dwelt an old woman who many of the ignorant and superstitious villagers called a witch. She had no magical power, but she knew the way of healing, and she had far more common sense and wisdom than most other people. But the people of the village were wary of her and, because of their taunts and slander, she decided to live alone in the forest.

Many of the villagers kept sheep and many of the boys of the village cared for their family's sheep while they grazed in the small valleys and on the hillsides nearby. Kirmin was one such boy. He cared for his parent's sheep and was well known throughout the village as a good shepherd.

One day Kirmin and his flock came to an open meadow where the grass was thick and a stream ran below the nearby cliffs. As soon as the sheep saw the lush grass they started to graze. Kirmin sat down in a shady spot and began to play his flute.

Usually after the sheep had been grazed and watered, Kirmin counted them and then tapped loudly with his stick, signaling the sheep to follow him home. This day, though, when he counted the sheep there was one missing. Kirmin knew that it was one of the lambs born only a week ago. He searched and searched but couldn't find the lamb anywhere. Finally, he went home, disheartened over the loss. He told some of his friends about the loss and after the rest of the flock was secured, they went back to the grassy field and began to search again.

More than an hour passed before one of the boys saw the young lamb, eating at the top of the cliff, munching away on the yellow blossoms that the sheep in this village loved to eat. The boys shouted and called, played their flutes and tapped their sticks, but the young lamb ignored the world around it and continued to eat. Kirmin began to cry. He knew how much his family depended on the flock for their livelihood and he loved each one of the sheep, especially the foolish young lambs. He knew that if he could not get the lamb home by nightfall then it might freeze out on the cliff top or, worse yet, fall prey to a wild animal. Neither he nor his friends could figure out what to do until one of them suggested asking the old witch for help.

"Go to her Kirmin. She can use her magic to get the lamb down."

"That is a good idea" said Kirmin. "Let's all go together."

The other boys backed away. "We're not going near that woman. She might turn us all into something awful. Its your lamb, you go." With that, the boys turned and walked quickly back to the village.

Kirmin looked up to the top of the cliff again and saw that the lamb was no longer eating, but was now bleating pitifully, finding itself all alone and high above where the other sheep had grazed. Kirmin decided to risk everything to save the lamb and turned and ran toward the old woman's hut.

"Mother witch," he called, as he knocked on the door. It slowly opened at his touch, and there, lying on a mat, was the old woman, sound asleep. "Old mother witch, please get up and help me," he cried.

The old woman opened her eyes and quickly sat up. She was angry at the intrusion and angry at the name he was using to address her, but when she saw the young boy's face stained with tears and frightened, her anger faded.

"What is the matter my son?"

Kirmin told her about the lamb and asked her to use her magic to save it. The old woman laughed. It was not a wicked laugh, but the laugh of someone who knows the answer and is willing to share it. The old woman wrapped a tattered shawl around her shoulders and took hold of her walking stick. She handed Kirmin a rope and three pieces of cloth and told him to follow.

In a few minutes they were standing at the bottom of the cliff. She looked up and then to the left and right, and said, "Well it is certain that your lamb did not climb up onto this high cliff from where we stand so let us look around and find the path that it took to the top."

After a while they found a tiny and steep path, which wound its way upward among the rocks. It was a twisted and dangerous climb, but it was the only way the lamb could have taken to reach the yellow blossoms high above. The old woman told Kirmin to follow the path and see if it led to the top. When he shouted down that he could see the lamb and that the path led to the frightened animal, she called for him to return.

She handed him the rope and three pieces of cloth. "Now boy, take these with you. When you get to the top slowly crawl towards the lamb and slip the noose over its neck and back away leading the lamb away from the edge. When you are safely away from the edge pull the lamb close to you. It will fight you but you must be strong. Tie one of the pieces of cloth over its eyes and secure its feet with the other two pieces. Use the rope to fasten the lamb to your back and then climb down. Go slowly, using the rocks and grass around you to keep your balance. Forget the lamb on your back and pay no mind to its bleating and wriggling. You are a brave boy and soon we will be on our way home, safe and sound."

Kirmin did as he was told. He used a handful of the sweet yellow flowers to entice the lamb to come to him. First he blindfolded it and then he tied its legs, just as the old woman had told him to do. After he tied the animal to his back the most difficult part of his task lay before him. The climb down was much more dangerous with the weight of the lamb on his back but, Kirmin kept remembering that the old woman had told him he was courageous. Her words lifted his spirits and seemed to guide him down the cliffside.

Soon the young shepherd was safely down and the old woman hugged him and told him he was as brave as any warrior. They walked toward the village together. By the time they came to Kirmin's house it was dark and everyone was asleep except his mother. When he turned to thank the old woman, she had left his side and was gone, disappearing into the dark night.

He told his mother the whole story, how the old woman had been so clever and had helped him not with magic but with advice and encouragement. He bowed his head and said, "I feel ashamed that someone we have treated so badly was so happy to help me. She isn't a witch at all."

The next day the whole village heard the story. When Kirmin returned the rope and cloth, all of the villagers accompanied him. They too were ashamed of how they had treated the old woman and they thought of the years of scorn and abuse she had endured because of their prejudice. They joined their hands together and begged her forgiveness. They asked if she would return with them to live in the village and share her knowledge of life. Kirmin's mother offered her a place in their home. After all the years of loneliness, the old woman was only too happy to live among the villagers once more. Through her simple teachings, the old woman led the people around her away from the dark fears of superstition and prejudice and into the light of common sense and wisdom.

The wise woman, the misunderstood elder who has knowledge that others not only lack but also fear, was and still is the object of hate and ridicule. This is a beautiful story that shows what a little understanding can do to bring people together. It can be found in The Tales of India *by Daulat Panday.*

Chapter Four

Families

Baucis and Philemon

Ancient Greece

In the time when the gods walked among men and women, Zeus and Hermes traveled together through the countryside, visiting towns and villages and asking the people there for rest and shelter. The two gods found every door closed against them and no hospitality offered until, at last, they came to a small cottage on a hillside. Here, Philomen and his wife Baucis lived—two people who had married young, worked hard together through their middle years, and were now content to live quietly in each other's company in their waning years.

As Zeus and Hermes crossed the threshold of the little cottage, they found places set for them at the table. Warm water for bathing and towels for drying sat beside the hearth. While the gods rested, the two old folks who had opened their home busied themselves attending to their guests. The table was rubbed with fresh herbs until the aroma filled the cottage. Wine was brought from the cellar and olives, cheeses, breads, and eggs were laid out on the table. Soon, a hearty stew was placed before the two disguised gods. Even though Philomen and Baucis served the food and wine in earthen bowls and cups, the old couple shared what little they had, for long ago they had learned the art of being good neighbors.

As they ate and drank with their guests, Philomen and Baucis noticed that no matter how much wine the two men drank, the pitcher never emptied; the wine continued to flow. No matter how much food was consumed, more always covered the plates and filled the bowls. Soon, the old couple realized that these were no ordinary guests—they must be gods. Philomen feared that their meager offerings were not enough, so he tried to catch the old goose in the yard, wishing to kill it as a sacrifice to the two immortals. But time had taken away the old man's speed and nimbleness and, try as he might, the goose would not be caught.

Finally, Zeus spoke. "We have come down from Olympus to walk among men and none have shown us kindness or hospitality until we entered your cottage. Come. You must follow us now to the top of the hill."

The old couple followed Zeus and Hermes to the top of the hill. Stretched out before them lay a beautiful valley dotted with the homes of people who had barred the gods from their doorsteps. Zeus raised one hand and the whole valley, with all of its villages, was instantly covered in water. A vast lake now stretched from the hillside where Phimomen and Baucis lived to the mountains beyond. Not one person who lived in the valley had survived the destruction. At the same time, the humble cottage of Philomen and Baucis seemed to disappear as a beautiful temple to Zeus and Hermes took its place.

Zeus looked at the generous couple and spoke kindly. "The people below allowed themselves to forget about the courtesy and kindness owed to weary strangers, but you remembered. What reward would you like?"

Philomen thought for only a moment and then spoke quietly. "We would like to live out our days as the priest and priestess of your temple, bringing comfort to travelers. When our days are over, we pray to be blessed by dying together, for neither of us could bear the sorrow of watching the other pass away and living only to mourn."

Zeus granted Philomen's wish, and the kind couple took care of the temple for many years, happily treating all travelers as well as the gods had been treated. Then, on a sunlit morning, as their days were coming to an end, Philomen and Baucis sat outside the temple, telling this story to passing travelers. As the two of them were speaking, they began to change. At first, they grew taller. Then, tree bark slowly grew over their bodies and branches and leaves sprouted from their sides. Finally, as Philomen became a powerful oak, and Baucis, a graceful linden, they turned toward each other and, with their last breath, whispered, "Farewell, my beloved."

What a love story! What a way to spend eternity! Found in most collections of Greek myth but check out Diana Ferguson's Greek Myths & Legends.

The Father Who Went to School

Ukraine

There once was a man who had four sons. He lived to a great age and decided to divide his lands and money among them. He thought that he would pass his remaining days living with one or the other, enjoying his grandchildren and the company of his sons and their wives.

The old man went to live with his eldest son first. In the beginning this son treated his father with respect and was good to the old man. Sadly though, as time went on, the son began to resent his father and often shouted at him and treated him badly. The old man no longer had his own room and his clothes went unwashed and unmended. He no longer had the best of food but had to settle for scraps from the table. No one talked to him; no one cared if he was well. The eldest son was sorry he had ever asked his father to come and stay with him.

At last the old man had no choice but to go and live with his second son. Sadly, he only exchanged wheat for straw. The wife of the second son always complained that they had so little and now they had to share it with an old man. Soon he moved on to the third son, but it was the same and soon he moved to the house of his youngest but nothing changed. So, as you can see, the old man moved from one house to another and each of his sons, in turn, was eager to push the burden of the father onto the next brother. One brother had too many children, another too small a house, another was too poor, another was too busy, and none of them wanted the old man around. Too tired to argue, the father finally bowed his head and cried, telling them to do with him as they pleased.

The four brothers met and tried to come up with a plan that would relieve them of their burden once and for all. Finally, one of them said, "Let's send father to school. There will be a place on the bench and he can take something to eat in a sack. He'll be out of our sight and out of our way all day long."

The others agreed but the old man was horrified.

"My eyes are not what they used to be and you want me to try and read small little letters in a book? I never learned to write or read in my whole life.

How can I learn now? The teacher and the children will ridicule me for my ignorance and my age. Can't I just live out my life in peace?"

But the brothers were pleased with themselves and their ridiculous plan. The very next day they sent him off to school.

As he walked through the forest he thought of the humiliation he would have to suffer as a student and how he wished his sons loved him better. While he was lost in thought, a carriage rolled by and the old man respectfully stepped aside. The carriage stopped and the nobleman inside asked the old man where he was going.

"To school," said the old man.

"To school, grandfather? You should be at home with your loved ones enjoying the fruits of all your years of labor."

The old man started to cry and told the lord his story. By the end of the story the lord also had tears in his eyes and felt compassion for the old man. "School is not the place for a man of your years or wisdom. Let me help you."

He took from his belt a silk purse, the kind that a rich man might carry. He poured something into it until it was nearly full and then placed it into a wooden box that he had on the floor of his carriage.

"Take this box home with you and tell this story to your children." The old man listened carefully, smiling and nodding at the nobleman's words. When the kind man finished talking, the old man thanked him and walked back to his oldest son's house. The other sons were still there and, when they saw him, they stared at the beautiful wooden box, wondering what its contents might be. Curious and a bit anxious, they told the old man to rest his weary legs. They brought food and drink and finally asked him what was in the box.

The old man shared the story that the nobleman had instructed him to tell. "A long time ago, before any of you were born, I was young and took to the road to see a bit of this world. In my travels I made some money, a few gold coins here and some silver coins there. I thought that I would save this meager fortune for the future in case I needed it. I went into the forest, dug a hole, and buried it in this box. Afterwards, I was a prosperous farmer and had such good children that I never thought about the money again. But today, when you sent me to school, I was passing the old oak where it was buried and I dug it up. I have brought the treasure home with me and will keep it safe until I am about to die. Whoever among you treats me with the most kindness and generosity, then that son and his family will inherit the box and all its contents. The old man paused, looking at his sons. "Which of you will be kind to your old father now?"

As you may well imagine, the brothers and their wives nearly fell over each other as they begged him to come and live with them. And so, the father lived the rest of his years with his sons and their wives and their children. At each house he was well fed and treated in a way that was fitting for a person of his position and age.

When their father died, they gave their father a magnificent funeral and invited all the neighbors to a feast in his honor. The sons paid for the priest to say prayers for him for forty days.

When the feast was over the four sons brought out the box and prepared to open it while all the neighbors were watching. They had decided that since each of them had taken such good care of the old man in his last years then each one should have an equal share of the treasure. Upon opening the box, they found the rich silk purse. They shook it and it tinkled with the sound of their hoped for reward. The eldest brother untied the purse and emptied the contents onto the table. Shocked, all four brothers could not believe their eyes. The silk purse held nothing but pieces of broken glass.

Disappointed, embarrassed, and furious, the brothers began to shout and accuse each other of being fools. The neighbors all laughed at their anger and greed.

"See what you get for sending your old father to school," they said. "He was a long time in learning his lessons, but when he did he learned them well." Laughing at the son's foolishness, the neighbors all walked home and said a heartfelt prayer for a wise old man.

A bittersweet story about families and how greedy members get their just reward in the end. This tale is found in several cultures and can be found in The Magic Egg and Other Tales from Ukraine *by Barbara Suwyn.*

The Three Brothers and the Pot of Gold

Moldavia

Years ago there lived a farmer who had three sons. Now among farmers, having three sons should have been a blessing, but these three had little time for farm work. In fact, they had little use for work at all. All were strong, healthy and good young men. The only vice they had, and such a vice it was on a farm, was that they hated work. They were born lazy. When they were young they would sit under a tree and watch the leaves turn colors. They invited other children to visit and then watched them as they played with their toys. When they grew older they would watch the young women walk past their farm but were too lazy to ever go out and meet them. When they became young men, they talked endlessly about nothing and sometimes, when the mood hit them just right, they might go fishing. But, if they caught too many fish they might leave most behind, for it was too much work to carry them all home.

The neighbors would watch them as they stretched out beneath the trees in the yard and shake their heads.

"Why do you not help your father around the farm?" they called.

"Father enjoys his work and in his work he provides for us. Why should we work and deny him that pleasure?" The brothers would reply, laughing and eventually falling asleep.

The father tried his best to get them to work, but it was all in vain. The years went on and finally the old man wore himself out and was on his deathbed.

"My sons, the end to my work is near. Soon I will leave you and I fear so much for your future."

For the first time the three young men were roused out of their apathy. They exchanged worried looks. The oldest knelt by his father's side and spoke. "Father we need your counsel and your blessing. What are we to do?"

The father looked at his sons and slowly said. "My boys, when your mother and I were young we saved our money very guardedly. We knew that hard times might come again and send the wolf to the door. We tried to put one gold coin every month into a small pot that we buried in the yard. As the years went by and you boys came into our lives, we couldn't put any money away and quickly forgot about the pot of gold. I can't remember where, but somewhere in the yard or perhaps in the field next to the house there is a pot of gold. I hope you find it and that it saves you all." With these words the old man closed his eyes and died.

The three sons wept for their father and in their grief kept his memory alive in their hearts for a long time. But soon they were hungry and the little food and money that their father had in the house was soon gone.

"Our father spoke of a pot of gold," said the middle brother. "I say we start to dig around the house and try to find this gold and keep ourselves alive." The other two agreed.

For the first time in their lives the three brothers began to work. They shoveled and dug and dug some more. At the end of the first day their hands were blistered and their backs ached and the places where their muscles should have been were sore but they found no gold. They started anew the next day. All week they dug till the whole yard was dug up and the earth was rich and brown and still they found no gold. They dug even deeper and found nothing. Next they began to dig in the field next to the house. When they found large rocks and stones they dug them out and rolled them to the side to build fences with. Soon the field was dug, like the yard, rich and brown and still no pot of gold. The brothers looked around and the eldest spoke.

"It seems a shame to waste all this work. Let us plant a vineyard and a garden here and try our hands at a trade."

And so the three brothers planted a vineyard and they began to raise a small vegetable garden as well. The grapes grew well and they prospered.

One day as they sat on their porch after a hard day's work in the vineyard they sipped their coffee and looked out over their labors. Their grapevines were heavy with grapes and their vegetable garden kept their tables full and left them produce to sell.

"You know," said the eldest. "Our wise father did leave us a treasure after all."

They all agreed that he was a very wise man.

I first heard this story from my grandmother who was very fond of stories that taught me a lesson. She would usually tell me this one if I balked at helping her around the house or in the yard. I remember once when I had helped her for a short while to hang the clothes on the line in the backyard and then began to run through the sheets, head down like a young bull. I heard this story then and many, many other times.

The Grandfather and His Grandson

Portugal

Many years ago there lived a man and his donkey. They had farmed together, plowed fields and harvested grain together, gone to market together, and had grown old together. The old farmer also had a grandson who was more than the joy of his life. He knew that he was nearing the end of this days and he wanted to leave the boy a little something beside the tiny patch of land he farmed. The only other valuable thing he owned was his donkey, so he decided to sell it at the market and give the money to his grandson.

One morning as the old man got ready to go to the market, he called his grandson and asked if he would like to go along. The boy was happy to spend time with his grandfather, especially on market day.

"I am selling my donkey," said the old man. "I'm too old to farm and have nothing to bring to market, so I really don't need him. I know he's old, almost as old as I am, but I think he still has a few good years in him, and he might fetch a fair price."

"Since we are trying to sell the old boy, let's not ride him. It's a hot day and he'll look much better at the market if he hasn't been carrying our weight. We'll walk and talk at his side."

So they started on their way down the road, walking next to the donkey. But as they walked, they passed some farmers working in their fields. The farmers looked up and saw the old man and the boy and shook their heads sadly.

"That old man must be very mean. Here it is a hot day and he's making that poor little boy walk instead of letting him ride the donkey."

When the old man heard this he stopped and put his grandson on the donkey's back. Feeling better for his deed, he walked alongside.

After they had traveled for a while more, they passed some men digging a well near the roadside.

"Look at that boy riding the donkey while his poor old grandfather has to walk on such a hot day. Today's youth have no respect for their elders."

When the old man heard these words he stopped and took his grandson off the donkey and got on it instead. He and his grandson walked on for a few more miles this way until they met some people coming back from the market.

"Look at that old man," they murmured, "riding in luxury on the back of that donkey while the poor little boy walks beside him. There's no love there, I can tell you."

When he heard this the old man told the boy to get up behind him and they both rode into the village.

Once they reached the market place the grandfather and grandson walked patiently along while several carts pushed past them. Some of the vendors in the market looked at the pair scornfully.

"On a hot day like today! Can you imagine the two of them riding that old donkey? The poor beast looks as if it might collapse under their weight. What's wrong with the two good legs God gave them to walk on."

Several of the vendors teased and berated the old man for making the donkey carry such a heavy load in the heat of the midday sun.

Soon, the two of them got off the donkey and the jeers and complaints stopped.

The old man turned to his grandson and asked, "Well my boy, have you learned a lesson from all this today?"

Looking up, the boy listened as his grandfather said, "When you try to please everyone you end up pleasing no one. No matter what you do, someone will think you should have done otherwise. When you have to make a decision, Grandson, make sure you don't think of how it will please this person or that person. Always do what you think is right and it will always be best." Slowly, the two of them turned around and walked home, the donkey walking beside them.

As the story goes, the grandson had learned his lesson well. They say he grew up to be a strong-minded man who always did what he thought was right and was admired for it by all who knew him.

The old man never did sell the donkey and the two of them spent many more years together before they each passed on. Some folks who knew the farmer had intended to sell his donkey wondered if the old man had asked too much for it or if the animal was too far past its prime to bring a fair price. The answer may well be that the old man never really meant to sell his old friend. A donkey that can help teach such a powerful lesson, and shape a good man out of a boy, is too valuable to sell at any price.

Sometimes you win, sometimes you lose, and you can never satisfy all of your critics all of the time. This poor grandfather was right, though, not to sell that donkey. You can find a version in Folk Tales from Portugal *by Alan Feinstein.*

The Wooden Bowl

Germany

Once upon a time there was an old man. As the years took their toll, he went to live with his son and daughter-in-law. The old man tried to help as best he could around their farm feeding the chickens and tending to the garden. But his back was bent and sore and his hands often trembled even with easy work. His son and daughter-in-law had their first child soon after the father arrived and the old man was overjoyed at being with his grandson. When the boy was old enough his grandfather told him stories and sang him songs. He taught him to recognize wildflowers and birds and taught him how to make a kite. The boy loved his grandfather and the old man loved the boy.

As the months went on, the old man's hands trembled more and more and he began to spill his food onto the tablecloth and sometimes it fell from his mouth. His son and daughter-in-law were disgusted. Soon he was eating alone at a small table away from the family, away from his beloved grandson.

One day his trembling hands failed him and he dropped the clay bowl that he ate his meals from and it shattered on the floor. The son yelled at his father and was so upset that he gave his father the old wooden bowl that once held the seeds that the old man used to feed the chickens. The old man sighed and said nothing, accepting his fate with resignation.

One day the father and mother watched their son take a piece of wood from the woodpile. The boy took out the little knife his grandfather had given him and very carefully began to work on the wood, carving and shaping it very slowly as only a child can. The father sat near his son and asked him what he was making with the wood.

"I'm making a wooden bowl, father, so when you are old and your hands tremble like grandfather's you'll have something to eat out of at meal time."

The man and his wife looked at each other with tears in their eyes, tears of shame. They brought the old man back to their table where he ate with his family the rest of his days. And if he spilled a bit of food once in a while they smiled at him and gave it no thought, no thought at all.

A wonderful story I have heard for years from many tellers in many ways. Found in the Grimm Brothers' collection.

The Magic Forest

Croatia

Long ago an old woman lived with her son at the edge of an enchanted forest. One day the young man wandered into the forest and, feeling tired, sat down to rest. Looking down, he watched as a beautiful silver snake slowly moved from the shadow of a stump onto a tuft of moss. "What a lovely little snake," the young man said to himself. "Perhaps I'll take it home as a pet."

Suddenly the snake turned into a beautiful young woman with hair like gold. Softly she spoke, "You have freed me from a horrible spell." The young woman was careful not to open her mouth too far, for she really was a snake taking on human form and her tongue was still forked.

The man and woman walked all day though the enchanted woods until, as evening came upon them, he proposed marriage to her. He took her home and told his mother about his bride-to-be.

At first the old woman was delighted but when she saw the young woman she knew that something was wrong. The mother was wise in the ways of the world and of magic. She took her son aside and warned him.

"Be careful my son. This young woman may not be what she appears. I fear that the snake is still there inside of her."

Hearing this, the young man was outraged. Turning against his mother, he showered all his love and attention on his bride-to-be.

After they were married the new bride made life hard on her mother-in-law. She made her do all the chores and treated her unkindly at every turn. There was an evil light that seemed to shine from her beautiful eyes whenever she spoke to the old woman.

One cold winter's day the young woman turned to mother-in-law and said, "Go to the top of the mountain and fetch me some snow so I can use it to wash my face and keep myself young and beautiful."

"But I could fall climbing up that steep mountain," replied the old woman.

"And who would care?" laughed the wife.

The old woman was quiet. Arguing would do her no good. She feared that her son, who was now totally enchanted by his wife's beauty, would never go against her. As she began to walk the dangerous paths, she thought of praying for safety, but she knew her prayers would only bring God's attention to the sins of her son, so she remained silent. Still, it seemed as though some of her thoughts must have reached heaven and she returned home safely with her bucket of snow.

Weeks later, in the deepest, coldest part of the winter, the young wife felt a craving for fresh fish. "Go to the lake and catch some fresh fish for my supper."

"But I could fall through the ice and drown," the old mother cried.

"All the better," her daughter-in-law laughed and the son laughed with her.

She struggled through the snow to the lake and slowly started to walk on the ice that crackled and sang under her feet. She was so afraid the ice might give way and she'd drown that she almost prayed. But then she didn't want God to learn of her son's sins and she remained quiet. Just then a gull flew overhead, a large fish wriggling in its beak. The fish struggled free and fell right at her feet. She picked it up and took it home, much to the disappointment of her daughter-in-law.

A few days later she was mending some of her son's shirts, sitting by the fire when the young wife snatched the shirts from her hands.

"You are ruining his clothes," she scolded.

"Mind my wife, mother, or leave," the son told her. The old woman nodded and handed the rest of the clothes to the young bride. Then the old woman went outside and sat alone on the frozen porch, her needle and thread still in her hand.

A few minutes later a young woman from the village walked by, bent under a load of kindling. Her coat was torn and she shivered when the cold wind whipped at her. "I have some kindling to sell. Do you need any?" she asked.

"No dear child, but I see that your coat is torn. Please come here and let me sew that tear up and give you a bit more warmth on this cold day." The old woman quickly sewed the coat till it was as good as new.

"Thank you, mother," said the girl. She left behind a bundle of kindling as a payment for her patched coat.

That night the son and his wife went to dinner in the village.

"Have a hot bath ready for me when I return and feed the chickens and clean their coop as well," she ordered her mother-in-law. The young woman prided herself on her chickens and that they could lay eggs even in the middle of winter, even on the coldest day. (Of course no one knew she used magic, did they?)

After they had left, the old woman lit a fire and then went to the well to fetch water for her daughter-in-law's bath. As she walked back to the house she heard laughing and when she entered she saw twelve little men dancing around the kitchen. Their eyes sparkled like coals, their coats were as red as flames and their beards were gray like smoke.

"Who are you?" she demanded.

"We are fire elves," they answered and again started dancing, this time drawing the woman into their circle. Soon she was laughing and singing and clapping her hands to the beat of their tiny feet. She felt young again and laughed as she remembered how she loved to dance with her husband and how they would sing songs deep into the night. Then she remembered her son and the happiness and thoughts of her youth left her and she sat down, he head in her hands. The elves gathered round her.

"What's the matter? Don't you like our dance?" asked the smallest of all the elves. The woman explained about her son and the snake wife and how he had been enchanted.

The elves put their heads together and talked excitedly until the smallest one finally spoke, "We can put magpie eggs in the henhouse. Snakes love to eat young magpies. She won't be able to hide her true nature and your son will see for himself."

Just then the daughter-in-law and her husband returned home. The elves leapt into the air and disappeared in a cloud of smoke. The smallest one jumped into the fire.

"What was that?" demanded the snake wife.

"The draft from you opening the door just fanned the fire, that's all."

"What's that?" she asked when she saw the smallest elf in the fire.

"Nothing more than a stray coal probably moved by the draft," replied the mother.

The little elf could not control himself as he tweaked the nose of the snake wife as he flew through the air and out the door.

"What is going on here?" she said angrily.

"Just some chestnuts I put into the fire. You know how they pop and fly through the air sometimes."

The snake woman went in to take her bath while the elves went off into the forest to find some magpie eggs.

The day soon arrived when the new chicks were to hatch and the snake wife invited many of her neighbors to come over and witness this winter miracle. She had not checked the eggs so when the magpies emerged from their shells she could not control herself. She hissed and her forked tongued flickered out of her mouth as she slithered forward on her belly towards the young birds. The neighbors all screamed and ran for the door of the henhouse, crossing themselves and covering the eyes of their children.

"There you see now what your wife truly is!" cried the old woman.

Her son was still under the spell of his wife's magic. "All I see is a meddling old fool. I want you out of the house today."

Although she was heartbroken, the old woman knew it was time to leave. She was afraid to stay another night in her own home. She asked her son if she could wait until it got dark so her friends and neighbors wouldn't see her shame in leaving.

When the sun had set the old mother walked out the door with only some of her old clothes, some food and a small bundle of kindling to keep her warm through the night. As she crossed the threshold the fire in the hearth went out and the crucifix fell from the wall. In that moment, the veil that had clouded her son's thoughts and actions lifted.

"Oh, how could I have treated my mother this way?" But he knew he had been under the spell cast by his wife and now he was too afraid to confront her.

"Let us follow the old woman," he told his wife, thinking he might yet find a chance to save his mother and redeem his soul.

"Yes, we can watch her die," replied the snake wife, with a wicked flick of her tongue.

Deep in the forest the old mother stopped and built a small fire. As soon as the flames began to dance the twelve elves appeared and also began to dance, leaping and twirling around the fire. But when they saw the tears in the old woman's eyes they stopped.

"Why are you weeping, old mother?"

She told them how the plan had failed and how her son had made her leave her home.

The smallest one said, "Let's go to the Forest King and ask his advice. I'm sure once he's heard this sad tale he'll help."

One of them blew on a silver horn and a huge stag appeared. He blew again and twelve squirrels came running.

Then the elves put the old woman on the stag and mounted the squirrels, and they all rode far into the center of the woods where a huge oak tree stood. Inside the tree there was an entire village and a great castle made of gold.

The old woman and the elves entered the castle. There, seated on a throne, was the Forest King. They told him the story of the snake woman and her enchantments. He listened in silence. Then the Forest King looked at the old woman and pointed out the window of his castle to the village in the tree.

"Look," he commanded.

The old woman's eyes filled with tears of joy. This was the village of her youth. She saw her parents and her childhood friends. Down the lane came her husband as young and as sweet as the day he first came to woo her.

"All you need do is walk through the gate and clap your hands and you will be part of this village. You will be young again and young forever."

The old woman was filled with joy and she ran to the gate but then she stopped. "What will happen to my son?"

No one had noticed that the son and his snake woman wife had followed the old woman into the woods.

"Leave him to his fate," replied the Forest King.

The old mother turned away from the village. "No," she said. "No matter what he's done to me I won't forget my son. I can't leave him behind."

When the old woman spoke these words the forest seemed to shake and resound as if a great bell had been rung. The village disappeared. The Forest King bowed to the old woman. "You have chosen the life of another over your own joy. You have chosen pain over the delight of magic. Your love has broken the spell that binds the land and now the land is free."

The snake wife screamed and became a serpent once again, and slithered away into a hole in the earth, a hole that swallowed her up. The old woman looked around and the Forest King and the fire elves were gone, and she was alone in the woods with her son. He begged her forgiveness but she knew he had been enchanted.

"There is nothing to forgive," she said, and arm in arm they returned home together.

When winter ended and spring came again to the land, the son fell in love with the young woman who sold kindling. They married and lived happily with the old mother who soon had grandchildren to keep her busy, and they all found the magic that grows in a house such as theirs.

I first heard this story from my grandmother who often would tell this one in the spring—I never knew why and as a child I failed to ask. She sometimes asked at the end of the story if I would treat her the way the ungrateful son did for most of the tale. Never, Noni.

Chapter Five

Justice by Accident

The Rooster and the Hen

Albania

As the storytellers say, "Once there was, once there was, and once there was not" an old man who had a rooster and his neighbor, an old woman, who had a hen. Each day the hen laid an egg and each day the old man would go to the old woman and ask if perhaps that day he could have an egg, but she always said "no" and sent him away. Finally, he looked at her and said, "The day will come when you will want something from me and I'll remember the way you have always turned me away." The old woman just laughed.

One day the old man looked at his rooster and said, "Can't you lay an egg or give me something that I can eat or sell?"

The rooster said not a word but hurried off to perch on the garden wall of the king's palace. The rooster stood there and began to crow. He crowed and he crowed and he crowed, from before dawn until midday. Finally, the king had had enough. He ordered his servants to lock the rooster up in the treasury where the walls were thick and there were no windows, and, there was only one massive oak door. No one could hear the rooster now.

Finding himself alone in the treasury, the rooster walked over to a dusty bag, pecked at it until it opened, and started swallowing the small gold pieces that he found inside. He ate one piece, then ten, then twenty, then more. Once he had eaten his fill, the rooster lay down among the gold and jewels and pretended he was dead. When the servants found him, they threw him out on the garbage pile. The rooster immediately walked off and went to the old man.

"Old friend," said the bird. "Hang me head-down and shake me and shake me again."

The old man picked up the rooster by the legs and hung the bird head first and shook him. As he did this, gold coins began to drop from the rooster's mouth, first one, then ten, then twenty, then more. The man went from being very poor to being quite wealthy in a matter of minutes.

The woman who lived next door heard about his good fortune and asked the old man for a gold coin.

"When I asked you for an egg you always sent me away and now you will learn how it feels to be refused by a neighbor."

Now, the hen was eager to please her mistress, so she went to the rooster and asked him how he came to lay gold coins for his master.

"If you wish to lay gold coins," said the rooster, "you must eat the poisonous serpent that lurks at the edge of the village between the fields and the forest."

The hen went hunting for the serpent and ate it whole. She then went back to her mistress and told her to hang her upside down and shake her and she would give her gold coins.

The old woman hung the hen upside down and shook her. Out came the snake and bit the old woman and swallowed her down.

My grandmother loved tales that had just the right amount of "just" revenge. She really got a twinkle in her eye when she came to an ending that gave the bad neighbor or evil relative their just reward. You can find a version in Tricks of Women & Other Albanian Tales *by Paul Fenimore Cooper.*

I'll Roast You and I'll Toast You

Scotland

Once a long time ago there was an old woman who lived all alone in her little cottage in the hills of Scotland. Now, since she lived all alone and she was quite old, she often talked to herself, just for the company, of course. The folk in the nearby village told all sorts of stories about her, saying she was an old witch and claiming she had a treasure hidden in her house. You know, the kinds of tales that come from people with little knowledge of their subject and too much time on their hands. One day three tough-looking men were sitting in the pub, drinking and listening to the local gossip. They were ruffians who traveled the roads of Scotland looking for trouble and easy money. When they heard some of the stories about the old woman, they decided to kill her and take her money. Their leader was an evil-looking man with only one eye. It would not be the first time these men had robbed and killed.

That night the sweet old thing decided she would roast some kippers, some dried herring. Now she cooked the old-fashioned way with a brander, an open griddle that she used over the fire in the fireplace. She sat in her rocking chair and rocked away as she roasted her kippers and talked to them just as if they understood every word she spoke.

Now the three robbers were outside her door while she was cooking her kippers. They decided that one would come down the wide chimney, surprise her and unlock the door for the other two. The first man slowly lowered himself down the chimney but when he was halfway down, he heard her voice.

"There's three of you but not for long and one of you soon will be gone, for I'll roast you and toast you and eat you down."

The robber in the chimney didn't know she was talking to her kippers, but he did remember hearing the stories that she was a witch, so he clamored up the chimney and practically fell off the roof. He ran to his friends hiding behind the hedge. "She knows I'm coming down the chimney. She says she's going to eat me. And that's not all, she knows there are three of us. I heard say it. 'There are three of you but not for long and one of you soon will be gone, for I'll roast you and toast you and eat you down.' "

And then she laughed. "I'm not going to rob her or even enter that house." With that, he turned and ran down the lane as fast as his legs could take him.

His two friends watched him go in complete amazement. "He's gone soft," said the second one. "She's nothing but an old lady. I'll go down the chimney."

So he climbed onto the roof and slid slowly down the chimney.

Halfway down, he heard her voice. By this time she had put the second kipper on her brander. "There's one of you away, but the second one is yet to come. What a tasty morsel. I'll toast you and I'll roast you and I'll eat you down."

Now when the robber heard this he said to himself, "It's true; she is a witch and she knows I'm here." He climbed out of the chimney as fast as he could and ran to his one-eyed friend. "She's a witch, alright. She knew that one of us had gone and that I was coming down the chimney. 'There's one of you away but the second one is yet to come. I'll toast you and I'll roast you and I'll eat you down.' I heard her say it. She knows we're here. I'm leaving." He ran down the lane, stumbling over his feet as he went.

Now the one-eyed man was made of sterner stuff and thought that he'd seen it all. He just shrugged the words of the other two off as cowardice. He climbed up onto the roof and lowered himself down the chimney. Just as he did, the old dearie began to roast the last kipper and, as luck would have it, this last kipper was just like the last thief, it was missing an eye.

"Oh my, aren't we having fun? Come on, I'm just waiting for you. The other two are gone and you are next, you one-eyed darling. I'll toast you and I'll roast you and I'll eat you down."

"How can this be? She knows I'm here and she can even see me with my one eye." He rose out of that chimney like a spark from the fire and ran just as fast down the lane. Inside the cottage, the old woman smiled, talking to her last kipper until it too was done and she ate it down.

Perhaps the evening's events cured the three men of their wild and wicked ways. Just think, changed for life because of the words spoken by an old woman as she prepared her dinner.

This delightful story of a total breakdown in communication and understanding is found in many cultures. You can find a version in Kathleen Ragan's book Outfoxing Fear.

A Debate in Sign Language

Once a long time ago there was an evil bishop who hated the Jews. He schemed and he planned on ways to destroy them all or to drive them from his city. One day he called the leading rabbi of the community and said to him that he wanted to have a debate with a Jew, using signs only, no words. He told the rabbi that he had one month to find someone who would debate him. If he failed to find someone, all the Jews would be killed.

The rabbi called upon all the learned men in the community, but no one had the courage to face the bishop in debate. For three weeks, the people said prayers of deliverance in the temple but, by the beginning of the fourth week, no champion had come forward.

Then, a peddler returned home, a man who wandered from village to village selling his vegetables and eggs. He had been away for some time, and when he returned his wife and children were praying and crying.

"What's the matter? What has happened?" he asked.

"The wicked bishop has challenged one from our community to a debate with no words, only signs. No one has the courage to confront him, and if there is no champion, then we will all be put to death."

The peddler smiled and said to his wife, "Tell the rabbi that I will do it."

"But all the learned men are afraid of him. Why will you succeed?"

"I may not, but since we'll all be killed anyway, I may as well try."

The man and his wife went off to see the rabbi, who blessed the man for his courage and asked God to give him vision and wisdom.

The bishop was told that a Jew sent by the rabbi was there to debate him.

The room was filled with an audience of the bishop's clergy and Christian scholars only and the rules of the debate were laid out. Not one word could be spoken until the bishop determined that the debate was over.

The two faced each other and the bishop pointed one finger at him. The man answered by pointing two fingers at the bishop. The bishop reached into his pocket and took out a piece of white cheese. In reply the peddler took an egg from his pocket. The bishop threw seeds all over the ground. The peddler took one of his hens and set her down to eat the seeds.

The bishop was amazed. "You are a wise man indeed. You answered every one of my questions perfectly. Now I know how wise the Jews are, that even a humble peddler was able to answer me correctly." He gave the Jew gifts and a new coat to wear home.

When the people of the city saw the peddler leave the bishop's palace with gifts and a fine new coat, they praised God for their deliverance. The peddler was carried back to the synagogue on the shoulders of a happy, thankful crowd.

The rabbi asked the peddler, "How was it? Were the questions hard? Tell us what went on in there."

The peddler said, "The bishop pointed a finger at me, meaning he'd take out my eye if I answered incorrectly, so I pointed two fingers at him, letting him know I'd take out both his eyes. Then he took out a piece of cheese to show that while I was hungry he had food. I took out an egg to show him I had no need of his charity. Then he spilled some grain on the floor, so not wanting to waste it, I let my hen eat it up."

While the peddler was telling his story, the bishop was telling his side to those he had assembled for the debate.

"That man is wise. I pointed one finger at him, meaning there is only one king, but he pointed two fingers at me to remind me that there are two kings, the one on earth and the one in heaven. Then I took out a piece of cheese to ask if it was from a white or black goat, while he took out an egg to challenge me if it was from a white or brown hen. Then I scattered seeds on the floor to show that Jews are scattered all over the earth. The peddler then freed his hen, which ate up all the grain to prove to me that the Messiah will come and gather all the Jews to Israel from the four corners of the earth. Such wisdom."

So the Jews of the city were saved and the bishop became an admirer of their wisdom, found even in the most humble of peddlers.

––––––––––––––––

This story is found all over the world in many traditions. The wise are always found to be not so wise, and the humble rise up in the most unusual ways. A wonderful version can be found in the book Folktales of Israel *by Dov Noy.*

The Widow and the Fishes

Java, Indonesia

Years ago and far away on the island of Java, there lived a very poor woman. She had little to eat or drink and her clothes hung about her like rags. When she was able to find work she was so weak from hunger that she struggled to finish her chores. Often, all she could do was wander the forests and pick up sticks for firewood and trade them to her wealthy neighbor for a little rice. Worst of all, she was alone in the world, and all of her neighbors were wealthy and cared little for her condition.

The shack where the poor woman lived was run down and leaned heavily against the wall of one of her neighbors. The roof was full of holes and when it rained, there was no way to keep the water out. Added to all of her misery was the fact that she had never heard of Allah, so even the hope of prayer was denied her.

One day, as this lonely old woman was in the forest, trying to gather firewood but finding herself almost too weak to carry a single stick, she heard voices. She looked around and there, in a small muddy puddle she saw several little fish all huddled together. They had been caught away from the nearby pond and now were trapped by the dry weather. At first the woman was delighted, for she saw in those fish a chance for some dinner, but as she drew closer she realized their pitiful fate. Then she heard them chanting, led by a larger fish, "Allah, Allah! Send us rain or we will die!" Over and over again they chanted, looking up at the sky. The old widow was so struck by their prayer that she did not seethe dark clouds approaching, not until the rain began to pour down, filling the puddle with water that flowed into the pond, carrying the fish with it and from there into the river where they were safe.

The old woman was so impressed that she walked home thinking to herself, "If this Allah can send rain for the fish then certainly He can send me the money I need to eat and take care of myself." When she arrived at her little shack she sat in the middle of the floor and began to chant, "Allah, Allah! Send me money or I will die." She repeated this prayer hour after hour until her neighbor screamed at her to be quiet.

"Stop! Allah will not send you money. Allah is not listening. You are crazy and you are driving me crazy."

But the woman in her need still chanted and prayed. Hers was the prayer of the innocent who has nothing left to lose and so finds complete faith in God.

After the third day of listening to the poor woman's chanting, her angry neighbor took a sack and filled it with stones and broken pieces of glass, chards of clay pots and pieces of rusting iron. That night, while the woman rested, he leaned out of his window and dropped the bag through one of the many holes in her roof. It landed right on the sleeping woman and knocked her so hard that she was unconscious until late the next morning.

When the poor woman woke and saw the sack beside her, so absolute was her faith in Allah that she knew it was the money she had asked for in her prayers. She clasped her hands together and cried, "Thank you, Allah, for this gift. Now I will never go hungry again." Then she opened the sack and gold and silver coins spilled out onto the floor.

When the other villagers heard of her wealth, most of them were happy for the old widow. But the village headman, knowing her story and fearing for her safety, advised her to move to a distant city, which she did. True to her faith, her door was never closed to any one in need.

When her neighbor heard of the miracle he knew that he deserved the wealth also. Wasn't it he who filled the sack with rubble and hurled it onto the old woman? Shouldn't he get something? He decided to fill two sacks with stones, and broken glass and chards of pottery. He chanted and prayed to Allah all day for three days. "Allah send me money or I will surely die." On the third day he commanded one of his servants to climb onto his roof and tear a hole in it and throw the sacks down on top of him. The servant was shocked, but the miser threatened to beat him if he didn't do what he was told. The first sack hit the man in the head and knocked him out while the second sack broke both of his legs.

When he woke, he was in terrible pain, but he greedily opened the sacks. All he found was the rubble he had put in them himself. He screamed and cried at life and its lack of fairness.

Because of his injury he could no longer work, and so his servants abandoned him. Soon he was as poor as the old widow had once been.

This is a story from Indonesia about faith. Even though the woman did not know who Allah was, she had faith in what she had witnessed. What a gift! There is a beautiful version in The Magic Crocodile & Other Folktales from Indonesia *by Alice Terada.*

The Twelve Months

Greece

Once upon a time there was an old woman who went out to the woods to gather herbs. As she picked this herb and that flower she wandered deeper into the woods until she came upon a cave set against a cliff. Inside the cave she saw twelve young men sitting in a circle.

Looking up, one of the men called out to her, "Grandmother would you please settle an argument for us? We are the twelve months of the year and we want to know which one of us is the most beautiful?"

The woman laughed and said, "You are all beautiful. Each of you makes me smile in a different way. January and February bring the snows that cover the hills in white blankets, while March and April bring the rain that glistens on the branches of the trees and nourishes the budding plants. May and June bring the end of spring and the beginning of summer, while the sunshine of July and August fills our homes with the goodness of the vine and the field. September and October bring cool breezes from the sea while November and December herald another winter, with hoary frosts that greets us each morning."

"Grandmother, you have praised us all and we will reward you in kind. Please, give us your shawl." She handed it to them and they folded it and tied it and filled it so that she had to carry it over her shoulders.

"Thank you, kind sirs," she said when they gave it back to her.

When the old woman arrived home she gathered her family around her and told them of her meeting with the twelve months. Then she untied the shawl and out poured gold coins that filled the table and spilled out onto the floor. The old woman and her family could not believe their eyes. Their poverty was over and they would be free from hunger.

One day, a neighbor came by and remarked to the old woman that she and all her family seemed uncommonly prosperous of late. The woman told her about all that had happened in the wood—the forest cliff, the twelve months, and the shawl filled with gold. Now, this neighbor was always a bit envious of anyone else's good fortune and was more than a bit selfish and mean-spirited, too. She decided that she also must have some gold and so she walked into the woods and came to the cave in the cliff. There were the twelve young men and when they saw her they asked, "Grandmother, can you settle an argument for us? Which month of the year is the most beautiful?"

The woman thought for a moment and said, "None. The winter months are cold and snowy and chill my bones, while the summer months are hot and humid and make me tired. The spring months are rainy and muddy, and make it hard to walk to town, while the fall months are chilly and only get chillier."

"Very well, then," said the twelve young men. "May we have your shawl?"

She had brought a very large shawl and handed it over to them with excitement. They filled it up to the top and handed it back to her.

"Thank you," she groaned as she hauled the heavy shawl over her shoulder and turned toward home.

At home she gathered the whole family around the kitchen table and told them all of what happened. "And now we will be rich like our neighbors," she said and with that she opened the shawl, but the only thing that spilled out was dirt.

Filled with anger, the disappointed woman ran to her neighbor's house and complained loudly that the advice she had been given was bad.

Amazed, the kind old neighbor asked, "What did you say when the men asked you which month of the year was the most beautiful?"

"I told them the truth as I see it; none of them is beautiful to me."

"Well then," laughed the wiser and richer neighbor. "They rewarded you according to your answer."

I'm not sure whether it was too much honesty or a lack of tact that proved to be the neighbor's downfall. When faced with magic one must proceed with caution. A version can be found in Folktales of Greece, *edited by Georgios Megas.*

The Devil's Grandmother and the Two Butchers in Hell

Germany

Long ago, in a certain village there lived two butchers. As fate would have it, and she usually does, the honest man was as poor as a church mouse while the other man cheated both his neighbors and strangers alike, and grew fat and wealthy. After a while the poor man couldn't compete with the dishonest man and was so heavily in debt that he was forced to close his shop. Sometimes, when he was tired, or busy, or bored, the wealthy butcher would ask the poor man to come along and help out in his shop.

One day the old rascal called on the poor man to work for him making sausages. The poor man worked all day, from sun up to sun down with hardly a break. When the work was finished, the rich butcher gave him one small sausage for his pay.

The poor man was outraged and finally found the courage to speak. "When I had a shop I always rewarded my assistants better than this."

"And look where it got you," said the wealthy man. "You have no shop and you have no assistants. Learn a lesson by this." Laughing, he turned away.

The poor man stood his ground. "You really intend not to give me more? You have a huge pile of sausages that I made for you and if you gave me a few more you wouldn't miss them at all."

At this the rich butcher lost his temper. He reached into the pile of sausages, grabbed one, and threw it at the poor man. Then the cheat roared in a voice that the whole village could hear, "Here, take this and go. Now you have twice as many as before and you deserve none at all. Leave me in peace and go straight to hell."

The poor butcher left the shop and walked through the village, a beaten man. People stared at him in pity and he avoided their glances by looking down at the ground.

He walked past his humble cottage, past the edge of the village, and into the deep woods that covered the countryside. He stopped only long enough to pick up a stick so he could hang his two sausages over his shoulder like a tramp's bundle.

He walked and walked and walked, and finally decided that he would go just where the rich man had told him to go, hell. For what else could he do? There was nothing left for him in this world. The journey was long and by the time he stood in front of the gates of hell he had eaten one of the sausages. The gates were closed, so he knocked loudly. Before long an old woman came to the door and opened it. Now, at first sight she looked like anybody's kindly old grandmother with a twinkle in her eye, glasses down on her nose, and her knitting in her hand. But upon closer examination, you could see the hint of two small horns, peeking out from beneath her headscarf. The doorkeeper was the devil's own grandmother.

"What do you want here?" she asked. "We don't see a lot of people coming down here of their own free will."

The poor man said, "I am so poor that I have nowhere else to go." He told her his story from beginning to end. "Since my dishonest colleague sent me here, well, here I am. Please, I'm so cold after my journey just let me warm myself for a while near the fires of hell. Please, if you let me stay I will give you this sausage. I made it myself and it is rather good, if I do say so myself."

"Well," said the devil's grandmother, "I really don't know what to do with you. You are much too good to be spending any time in hell. You are shivering with the cold and you have been so kind to give me this sausage. I guess you can come in and warm yourself, but I'll need to hide you soon. The young devils will be coming back from tormenting people throughout the world and they will be starving, and who knows what would happen if they found you."

The butcher warmed himself near the fires of hell and the old woman gave him a nice supper of potatoes and goat's meat. They sat and talked, and he made her laugh with his silly stories.

When evening came the devil's grandmother hid the poor butcher in her room. Soon the young devils were back from tormenting people and were demanding their supper. As soon as they had eaten their fill, they all fell asleep, each by his own little fire, smelling of sulfur and brimstone. The sound of them snoring could wake the dead but not the poor butcher. He slept the sleep of an honest man that had a full stomach and a warm backside. He slept until mid-morning, when the young devils had already left for their day of tormenting the men and women of the world.

"I guess I can't really stay here but I want to thank you for making me more welcome in hell than I have been on earth." He gave the old woman a hug and turned to go.

"Believe me, you will not do so badly now, even in the world up above. Get along home and you'll find things improving at every step and turn." Saying this, the old woman handed him a whisker from the devil's own face. "Here," she said, "Take this as a keepsake and look after it like the eyes in your head, for it will bring you good luck." Then she handed him a package wrapped in white linen.

The poor man wondered how a whisker that smelled of brimstone could be a lucky token, but he carefully slipped it into his coat pocket and, waving farewell, left hell and began his journey home.

When he reached his little cottage the first thing he did was lay the old woman's gift on the kitchen table. He had noticed that it had become heavier and heavier as he walked home. When he unwrapped the bundle, there was a bar of solid gold, more wealth than he could ever earn in a lifetime.

The happy man decided to open another shop and this time he prospered. All the people who had been cheated over the years by his rival were happy to trade with the honest butcher. He built a new cottage and married a fine woman.

But, the honest man's good fortune was salt in the crooked man's eyes. The cheat could not sleep; he was so filled with envy. When he finally heard the story about the sausages, and going to hell and getting the magic whisker, he could not contain his greed. The next day he bundled up a huge load of sausages and headed straight for hell.

The devil's grandmother was knitting by the gates of hell when the rich butcher came knocking.

"Now," she said, "where are you going with that sack full of sausages?"

"I've brought these fine sausages here for the devils themselves to have for their supper."

"Are you going to give an old woman a taste of your fine meats?"

"You'll be lucky to get any leftovers. I brought these for the lords of hell themselves, not for an old gatekeeper who spends her time knitting."

"Well, you might as well come in and wait," she said. "The young devils should be home any time now." So the devil's grandmother opened the gates and let the greedy man into hell.

Now, the crooked butcher never returned from his trip to hell. Some say the young devils ate him up, along with the sausages, but I think they kept him down there to work as their butcher, grinding and stuffing countless sausages for all eternity.

I guess everyone has a grandmother, even the devil himself! At least it seems she has a better sense of fair play than her grandson. A version of this folktale can be found in Dragons, Ogres, & Wicked Witches *by Milos Maly.*

The Old Traveler

Estonia

Once so long ago but it seems like yesterday, not your yesterday but someone's, a poor old man traveled along the road. Night was coming on and with it the cold and damp that chills the bones. Now in those days, travelers were welcome to sleep by the fireplace or in the barn. Kindness was the rule not the exception.

The old man saw an imposing house up on a hill and thought that the people who lived there might spare him a place to spend the night. He walked to the front door and knocked.

Now the woman who lived there was rich and she was miserly. Her face was tight as if all the meanness inside her was trying to come out. "What do you want?"

"Kind woman can you give me shelter for the night—a place by the fire or in your barn?"

"Give your kind shelter? I'll let the dogs loose, that's what I'll do. Now off with you."

The old man understood and he moved on. At the bottom of the hill in the bend of the road he came to another house, this one a humble cottage. From inside the old traveler could hear singing and laughter and he knew this was a house filled not with wealth but with joy. Perhaps here, he thought.

He knocked at the door. A young boy opened it. "What can I do for you, grandfather?"

"Please could you give me shelter on this cold night, perhaps in your shed?"

"Come in grandfather Spend the night inside with my mother and brothers and sisters." The boy led the old man into the small cottage. "Mother we have a guest."

The children gathered around the old man, laughing and singing. They took his damp coat and hung it near the fire to dry. The children carried on entertaining the old man. Their clothes were ragged and threadbare. The furniture was old and had been fixed many times. The floors were bare but the children and the house were clean, just poor.

"How did you come to be this way?" asked the old man.

"My husband died a few years ago. We couldn't keep the farm so we sold it to the woman on the hill. First one child then another became ill. I used to sew clothes for all the people in the villages and farms around here, but now we can barely feed ourselves, let alone buy cloth to make new clothes."

"We have some food left from supper. It's not much."

The old man had bought bread and cheese and sausage that morning. "I've already eaten," he lied, "so you and the children can have some of my food." He reached into his pack and brought out his feast and shared it with her and her children.

The old man was spreading out his sleeping clothes near the fire when the boy who had let him in stopped him. "Grandfather, you sleep in my bed tonight. I couldn't sleep knowing you were here on the floor." And so the old man slept in the boy's bed and the boy slept by the fire.

In the morning the old man had some hot tea and toast and thanked the woman and her children. She walked him to the gate and as he turned to leave, he said to her, "I have a gift for you."

"I didn't give you shelter for a gift," she said.

"I know that—if you had I wouldn't be giving you a gift. That which you do first thing this morning you will do all day." He waved and smiled and walked away.

She smiled at his strange words and went inside. She went straight to her box where she kept her cloth and thought to herself that she might make a scarf or vest for one of the children if she had enough cloth. When she reached into the box, she didn't find a scrap of cloth. Instead she found silk—yard after yard after yard of silk—all the colors of the rainbow. And when the silk had filled the cottage up to their knees she began to pull out cotton of beautiful patterns and colors—yard after yard after yard of cotton till it came to their waists. And then she began to pull out wool—strong, warm beautiful wool—yard after yard after yard of wool.

She turned to her son and said, "Go to our neighbor and borrow her measuring stick. I'm going to make clothes for you all." The boy ran off while his mother still pulled cloth from her scrap box.

The neighbor was annoyed by the boy's request. "What can your mother sew? She has no money for cloth."

The boy told her the story of the old traveler. The woman listened intently and gave the measuring stick to the boy.

The rich woman thought to herself that she had been a fool. She deserved to have that kind of luck, not her neighbor. She sent a servant out looking for the old tramp. When he found him the old man didn't want to return.

"If I come back without you," said the young man, "my mistress will take my wages from me and my position too."

The old man took pity on the young man and returned with him. As they passed the cottage, the sun was just going down and the last of the cloth was pulled from the box. The woman knew what a great gift the old man had given her. She could sew clothes for her children and begin to sell clothes to the people in the towns around her. She and her children would never be poor again.

When the old man arrived, the rich woman met him at the gate, bowing and smiling. She took him into her house, fed him a wonderful meal, and showed him to his own room with a soft bed and clean sheets. He stayed with her for three days, quietly eating and drinking and smoking his pipe as he watched her run her household. He heard her harsh words for the servants when she didn't know he was listening. He saw her kick the old lame dog when she didn't know he was watching. Each day she became more anxious for him to leave and give her a gift. Finally on the fourth day he set off on the road again. She walked him to the gate.

She couldn't contain herself. "Tell me grandfather, do I get a gift for my kindness?"

He turned and with a smile, both sad and sly and he said, "That which you do this morning you will do all day." With that he walked down the road.

The rich woman was so happy. She rushed into her house and ran up the stairs to her attic where she kept her money chest hidden. She would count her money all day and be so much richer by nightfall. She reached up into the rafters where the money chest was hidden and as she did so dust from the top of the box flew into her face and she sneezed.

And she sneezed again, and again, and again. Every time she sneezed the dust rose and she sneezed again, each time louder than the time before. She sneezed and she sneezed and she sneezed.

She sneezed and the chickens refused to lay eggs.

She sneezed and the cows stopped giving milk.

She sneezed and the horses ran away.

She sneezed and the dogs howled.

She sneezed and the servants covered their ears and ran off to their homes.

She sneezed and her barn fell down.

She sneezed and the windows shook and shattered and the walls of her house began to crumble. And so she sneezed till nightfall. And when she finally stopped sneezing the rich woman sat alone in the ruins of her once-fine house. The lesson was not lost on her.

This is yet another story I learned from my grandmother. She was very fond of telling me the "punchline" to a story weeks before she told me the actual story. With this one she would just look at me and pretend to sneeze. You have to love the oral tradition.

The Fountain of Youth

Korea

Once in a village deep in the mountains there lived an unusually kind, elderly couple. Since they had no children to help them in their old age, they cut wood and sold it to others in the village. Their neighbors admired the way the old couple patiently accepted their lot in life and the kindness they showed toward everyone they met.

Near the humble couple, lived another elder of the village who was childless, but unlike them, this man was a greedy and spiteful person. No one in the village except the old couple had a kind word to say about him.

One day when the kind old man was cutting firewood in the forest he heard the sound of a bird singing. He had never heard a song more beautiful and, pausing in his work, he sat down and listened as the bird serenaded him.

Much to his disappointment, his musical friend soon flew away. But the old man, hearing its song not far away, followed the bird. When he reached the tree where it had perched, it flew away again. Over and over, the old man followed the bird only to have it fly away singing and enticing him to follow. Finally, after hours of following the bird, the old man saw that it had perched on a tree that stood near a clear spring. The bird was singing more beautifully than ever.

The old man sat down under the tree to listen and this time the bird did not fly away but sat, happily singing to its new friend. The old man, feeling thirsty, knelt by the pool of water to drink. The water was cool and sweet, and the old man drank his fill.

Soon he was very relaxed, the way he felt when he was with friends and they had just had some good, rice wine. At once he began to feel drowsy, so he lay down his head and fell into a deep sleep.

When he awoke the sun was setting and darkness was creeping its way into the forest. He remembered following the bird and its song and drinking from the spring. He hurried toward home and soon came to the place where he had been cutting wood. It seemed as if his body was lighter and he noticed that his arms and legs felt stronger. He picked up the frame of firewood that he had cut and was surprised by how light it was. With a spring in his step, he followed the path toward his home.

Meanwhile, the old man's wife had become worried when he didn't return before dusk. She imagined accidents or wild beasts or thieves and soon she was beside herself with fear. She went next door.

"Neighbor," she said, "my husband has not returned from the forest and I am so worried. Could he have had an accident or fallen prey to wild animals or brigands?"

Instead of helping his neighbor, the old man simply dismissed her. "It's late and he probably was devoured by wolves or a tiger."

The old woman asked if he would go with her into the forest and help her look for her husband, but the thoughtless man refused and told her it was a waste of time. She went back to her cottage and was preparing to go alone in search of her husband when she heard him whistling as he often did as he neared his home. She rushed out to meet him and saw him walking through the darkness, his wood on his back.

Once they were inside and she saw him in the light, she couldn't believe her eyes. She stammered and tried to speak but nothing came out of her mouth.

"What is it dear one?" cried her husband. "What is the matter with you?"

"Is it really you?" she asked.

"Of course it's me. Why do you ask?"

"You are so young. There's not a single wrinkle on your face," she cried in amazement.

The old man put his hands up to his face and felt his skin. It was true. "So that's why I felt so strong."

"How did this happen to you?"

Her husband told her about the bird and its song, and how he followed it through the forest. He told her about drinking at the spring and falling into a deep sleep.

"That must be it," he said. "The water from the spring tasted so cool and sweet, and I felt so good after drinking it."

His wife looked up at him and said, "Everyone will laugh at us, an old woman and a young man living together. Do you think the water might do the same for me, husband?"

The next morning the two of them went into the forest to find the magic water. When they found the pool the old woman knelt beside it and drank her fill. Almost at once she began to grow younger. Soon she was a young woman, full of life and strength just like her husband. Filled with relief and joy, the couple walked back to the village.

When their greedy old neighbor saw them and heard about the magic that had made them young again, he was filled with jealousy. When they told him about the spring and where to look for it, he immediately set off to find it.

All afternoon the couple watched for their neighbor's return. When it grew late, they decided to go and look for him. As they neared the pool they heard the sound of a baby crying. As the spring came into view they saw the infant lying in the grass next to the magic waters.

"This must be our ill-tempered neighbor," the man cried. "He was so anxious to be young again. He must have had too much of the water."

Together, the couple laughed at what had happened.

Then, suddenly, the wife turned to her husband. "What about this baby?" she said. "We can't just leave it in the woods, and besides, we are in some way responsible for what has happened."

Smiling, her husband replied, "Let's take the infant home and raise him as our own."

"A wonderful idea," replied the wife.

The couple, now young and strong, worked harder than ever and through the years their child grew to be kind and caring, just like his parents.

The fountain of youth has been a dream in the corner of men and women's minds since the beginning of time. You can find a beautiful version of this story in Korean Folk & Fairy Tales *by Suzanne Crowder Han.*

Chapter Six

Magic and Wonder

Why Man Lives Eighty Years

Bosnia-Herzegovina

When God first created the world, He wanted each man and woman to live for only thirty years. "You will be the tsar of all creation," God told the first man and woman. "You will be beautiful, young, healthy, strong, and wise, and your life shall last thirty years."

Now man was happy to be the ruler over God's creation, but the idea of living only thirty years was not as attractive. Still, knowing God and all His wisdom, man said nothing.

Next, God created the donkey and said, "You will eat the most unappetizing food and you will never be satisfied. You will work for man and carry heavy loads, pull wagons, and carry men and women on your back. They will treat you unkindly and beat you for your shortcomings. You will live thirty years."

The donkey thought about what God had said and asked Him, "Lord, since I will have to suffer so much, thirty years seems like a long time. May I live only ten years?"

God smiled at the donkey's wisdom and replied, "Of course you may. You will live ten years."

When man heard what passed between God and the donkey he spoke up and said, "Lord, may I please have the twenty years that donkey does not want?"

God listened to man's request and said, "You may have those twenty years but you must take them as they are."

Man was happy because now he could live as God's ruler over creation for fifty years.

Then God created the dog and told him, "Whatever you have that is yours you must defend as long as you live. You will bark and sense danger when it is still far away. You will never rest because your senses will always alert you to danger. You will always do more for others than for yourself and your life shall last thirty years."

"Lord," replied the dog, "since I will lead a life that is full of anxiety and trouble, may I only live ten years?"

"If that is what you wish, then live just ten years," said God.

Again man spoke up and said, "Lord, if the dog does not want those twenty years, may I have them?"

"If you want them, they are yours," said God, "but only as they are."

Now man was looking forward to a life of seventy years.

Finally, God created the monkey. "You will look very much like man," said God, "but you won't be man. You will climb trees and swing from branch to branch to escape those who hunt you. You will imitate what others do and not know why you do so. You will live thirty years."

"Thirty years seems too long a life for such as this. Could I live no more than twenty?" asked the monkey.

"Of course," said God.

Again, man asked, "Lord, may I have the ten years that monkey did not want?"

"They are yours, but only as they are."

Now man was truly happy. His life was now eighty years long and stretched out before him, full of wonder and excitement.

Now, everything has happened to man just as God said it would. For the first thirty years of life, he is healthy, beautiful and young. Then, at thirty, he marries and raises a family, and he takes on the burden of the donkey as he toils to provide for them. At fifty, he guards what he has and worries about each possible danger, just like the dog. At seventy, a man often resembles a monkey, bent over, withered and brown with age, sometimes not really knowing why he does what he does.

His life is long, as he requested. Take care when you ask for more, as that may be just what you get.

This is another story that can be found in several cultures. You can find a version in Tales from the Heart of the Balkans *by Bonnie C. Marshall.*

Old Frost and Young Frost

Lithuania

A long time ago there lived Old Frost and Young Frost. Now, the younger Frost was a braggart and to hear him talk, you would think that the world was at his feet because he was so clever and strong.

One day Young Frost said to himself, "My father has grown old and weak and he does his work poorly. With my strength and wisdom I can freeze people better since no one can hide from me and no one can trick me."

Just to prove his point, Young Frost went off in search of someone to freeze. He flew high above the trees and the frozen lakes, high above the river and the frozen fields until he spied a lord, riding in his carriage, drawn by his well fed and finely groomed horses. The lord was a heavy man, wrapped up in thick furs, his legs covered by a warm rug and his hands tucked into fine woolen gloves.

Young Frost started to laugh, "Furs and rugs will not help you. My father might not have been able to freeze you because he is old and weak, but I will chill you to the bone and make your blood freeze in your body."

Then Young Frost flew up to the carriage and started to work his cold magic. He flew up the man's sleeve and under his blanket. He wormed his way into the fingers of his gloves and down the back of his fur coat. The lord cried out to his coachman, "Hurry and get me home or I'll freeze to death in this cold."

Young Frost laughed when he heard those words and bothered the lord even more. He blew on the lord until the man could not feel his hands or feet and his nose was red with the cold. The lord shifted this way and that in his seat, but Young Frost showed him no mercy as he chilled him again and again.

"Faster," cried the freezing man.

When the lord finally arrived at the his estate he was so near death that he had to be carried from the coach to his room.

Young Frost flew to his father and began to boast of his power. "Look at me, father. I am so strong that even with his furs and rugs and fancy carriage the lord was near death by the time he got home. You'll never be able to match my skills. You could never chill someone as big and strong as that lord. I think that your days are over as the King of the Winter and I am ready to take your place." With that, Young Frost laughed and flew up high in the sky.

Old Frost just smiled at his son's boasting words and caught up with him in an instant.

"My son," he said, "do not be so eager in your claims of power. It's true you froze that old lord in his furs and carriage, but let us see how well you do against a real challenge? Do you see that peasant driving his sled into the woods to cut down trees for firewood? He has only a threadbare coat and vest and old, worn out gloves and boots. If you can freeze him, I'll believe in your power and strength."

Young Frost laughed and answered, "Freeze him? Why, that will be no problem at all. I'm sure it will take very little of my cunning and power to freeze that old stick."

Young Frost flew up into the air and swooped down on the unsuspecting peasant. He caught him and began to tease him and taunt him and as he chilled him with his icy breath. He flew at him from first one side and then the other, from above and then below, but the peasant just hunched over the reins and kept driving his horse and sled. Young Frost nipped at the man's feet and crept into his old worn out boots and past his thin wool socks and soon the peasant's feet were almost numb. But instead of turning back, the man merely jumped off the sled and ran beside his horse, warmth filling his boots as he kept moving.

Young Frost was a bit perplexed, but he thought to himself, "I'll get him in the woods."

Once he came to the woods, the peasant took his axe and began to chop down one tree and then another. Young Frost gave him no peace. He caught him by the neck and crept down his coat and chilled his back. He nipped at his fingers and face, and swept into his lungs. But the harder Young Frost worked at chilling the peasant, the faster the man swung his axe and the more trees he chopped. After a while he even took off his coat and worked in his vest, the sweat pouring down his face. The more Young Frost tried to freeze him, the harder the peasant worked and the warmer he got. The man even took off his gloves, working harder still. When this happened, Young Frost realized that he himself was starting to get tired.

"I'll get you on the way home," he said with what felt like the last of his breath. Young Frost just then got an idea. He crept into one glove of the peasant's empty gloves and breathed into the other one. "Now" he laughed, "how will he get these on his hands for the trip home? I have frozen them stiff."

The man chopped and chopped and felt as if he had enough energy to chop the whole forest down that afternoon. Finally his sled was full and he decided it was time to go home.

Young Frost, who had waited patiently, saw the peasant put on his coat and walk toward the seat of his sled to put his gloves on. "Now I have you," cried Young Frost, peering out from a glove.

But the man, seeing his gloves were frozen stiff, just laid them on the ground and began to hit them with the flat of his axe. He smashed his axe onto the gloves over and over again, while Young Frost moaned and cried and finally flew out of the glove and, feeling more dead than alive, limped painfully back to his father.

The peasant drove home, urging his horse along and feeling quite happy to have a good day's hard work behind him.

Old Frost took one look at his son and smiled, "My boy, you seem worn out and sorely treated. What's wrong?"

"I have never been this tired. I tried with all my strength to freeze that peasant and he never gave in to my chills. In the end, he gave me a good beating. I don't understand it."

"Let this be a lesson to you. You may be able to freeze the fancy lords in their furs and carriages, but they live a life of ease and have forgotten about hard times and hard work. The peasants are tough and they are wise, and you will never get the better of them. It's a hard lesson but I'm sure you will never forget it."

And Young Frost never did.

Even the seasons and the elements learn from their elders. This is a wonderful story about wisdom but also one that tells us about the sturdiness and determination of the old world peasants. You can find a version in the book A Mountain of Gems: Fairy Tales of the Peoples of the Soviet Land.

Why Misery Remains in the World

Brazil

Once there was an old woman—a *very* old woman—who lived alone at the edge of the village in a small hut. Her only possession of value was a beautiful pear tree that grew in her front garden. As the years took their toll, she found it more and more difficult to climb the tree or to reach the best fruit. The children in the neighborhood had no trouble climbing the tree, so they took the best pears and left her the small ones, the rotten ones, and the old ones. She would scold them, but the thoughtless youths only teased her and called her Aunt Misery. Soon, everyone called her that.

One day a poor man arrived at her door and asked for a place to sleep. Old Aunt Misery invited him in, fed him, and gave him a spot on the floor to rest. The next morning, she made him coffee and shared the last of her bread.

The man thanked her and then said, "What is it you wish? I can grant you something in return for your kindness."

Old Aunt Misery thought and thought, and finally she smiled and said, "I wish that anyone who climbs into my pear tree will be stuck there until I allow them to leave."

"You shall have your wish," he said, and waved good-bye.

Not long after this, the pear tree again bore fruit. Soon, Aunt Misery heard the children from the village up in the tree, laughing and picking her pears. When she stood under the tree, they jeered and called her names, but when they tried to climb down, they found that they were stuck in the branches. Suddenly the name-calling became begging and crying. Old Aunt Misery listened for a long time. Then, finally, she told the boys that if they promised never to return, never to pick her pears, and never to call her names, she would release them. They were only too willing to make that promise, a promise that they kept. So, at last, Aunt Misery settled down to enjoy her pears and her peace and quiet.

The old woman's life was good for many years and then, one day, a woman dressed in black came calling at Aunt Misery's door. "I am Death," she said, "and your time has come. Follow me."

Aunt Misery had no intention of following Death.

"Death, I know it is my time, but could I have just one last wish before I follow you?"

Death nodded.

"I was wondering if I could have one last pear from my tree. Since I am old, and cannot climb the tree as I used to, would you please pick one for me from the top, where the best and tastiest grow?"

In a moment Death was up in the tree. She picked a pear, but then found herself unable to climb down. Just like the boys in the village, Death had fallen into Aunt Misery's trap. Death begged and pleaded, but Aunt Misery just laughed. She knew that she was safe as long as Death remained in the tree.

For many years, life went on but Death was absent from the world. The sick and injured could not die; the old became older and older and begged to go to the next life. Those who made their living because of Death, the gravediggers and coffin makers lived in poverty. Hospitals filled to bursting. The world was no longer a happy place.

Still this suited old Aunt Misery just fine. She was healthy and happy and had no intention of dying any time soon. Finally, when she realized that the situation was truly out of hand, Aunt Misery decided she would let Death climb down, but only on one condition. Death would have to leave Aunt Misery alone and not ever come back for her.

Death accepted Aunt Misery's terms and was soon back at work. And so it is that Misery will never die and will be in this world until its end.

This story is found in many cultures. Aunt Misery finds a way to cheat Death but also to find just a bit of happiness in this world. I do like the idea of Death being a woman. You can find versions of this story in Brazilian Folktales *by Livia de Almeida and Ana Portella and also in* Greedy Mariani & Other Folktales from the Antilles *by Dorothy Sharp Carter.*

The Haunted House

Holland

Once there stood a house near Dokken that was haunted. Every night, at the stroke of midnight, a terrible noise was heard coming from one of its bedrooms. No one would sleep there and few would even enter the room. The people who lived in the house had no idea what made the sounds or what had happened to cause the uproar each and every night. Since no one was brave enough to stay in the room through the night, the mystery remained unsolved.

One evening, a little old woman came to the door of the house. It had been raining for several days and the trees were dripping with water, the ground was soaked, and a small river ran down the middle of the street. The old woman was drenched through and through. She was so tired and so cold that she needed a place to warm herself and get dry. She knocked on the door, thinking that surely she would be turned away from such a grand house, but instead found herself ushered into the front hall.

An older gentleman came out and spoke to her. "Are you looking for a place to stay on this wet night, madam?"

"Yes, kind sir, I am," she replied.

"Would you be willing to spend the night in a haunted room? It's the only room we have that is not occupied at this time."

"Any room would be just fine, sir. I have no reason to be afraid of those who cross over from the other side."

He bade her follow him, but she hesitated. "I hate to drip rainwater all over your fine floors and staircase, sir."

"Never mind the water. If you can spend the night and explain the mystery of the haunted room, then I will reward you handsomely. A little water on the floor is the least of my concerns."

They walked up a wide staircase and came to the end of a long hallway. The man unlocked a great door and pushed it open. The old woman could see that the walls of the old house were quite thick and the windows were wide and tall. As she stepped into the room, she noticed that it was completely empty except for a bed that sat in the corner.

The gentleman of the house looked thoughtfully at the woman and inquired again, "Are you sure you'll be alright? You're not afraid?"

Laughing, she replied, "I am far too wet and weary to be afraid. I could use a towel to dry myself though."

"One towel? My dear lady, you shall have a stack of towels, and soft sheets and warm blankets, also. Would you like to get right to bed?"

"Yes, please," she answered.

The towels and sheets and blankets were brought to her and she dried herself and climbed into the bed. She was so tired that she didn't hear the rain on the roof or the wind clattering against the window. She slept through the night and all of the next morning. When she finally woke she saw the door opening slowly and then the head of a little girl peeking in.

The old woman looked at her and said, "Come in, little one. Don't be afraid."

"Are you the rain lady?" the child asked.

"Why, yes. I suppose I am. What a beautiful name you've given me. Thank you. And what is your name?"

"I am Annetje and I'll be four years old next week."

Just then, they heard voices in the hall and Annetje hurriedly said, "Oh, I have to go. That's my Grandfather and he told me never to come into this room." She ran out the door and down the hall.

The rain lady, having slept soundly, had forgotten all about the ghost. She dressed and slipped down the staircase. She found her host and thanked him for the night's lodging.

"Aren't you going to tell us what happened in that room last night?"

"Nothing, sir. I slept right through the night and heard no noises."

"You saw and heard nothing?" he asked. "Why, the racket was so loud in our rooms, we thought it must have been deafening to you in yours."

"Would you like for me stay another night?" the woman asked. "This time I won't be so tired and I'll be able to stay awake and see your ghost when it comes to visit."

The gentleman of the house was pleased that she would stay another night. He called for a maid to freshen her room and prepare her a late breakfast.

"You are my guest and will be treated as such," he said.

That day, the old woman relaxed in the library and talked to Annetje and the other children, telling them stories and testing them with riddles.

That evening, the woman went to bed early so she would be awake at midnight when the unearthly sounds started. After several hours of sleep she sat up in bed. The night was as black as ink, with no stars or moon in the sky, but the room was filled with a dim, blue light. Near the window, a figure was walking back and forth, as steady as a sentry on guard duty.

"Who are you, sir, and what are you doing in my room?" cried the old woman.

The ghost floated to her bedside and held up a hand. "Go back to sleep," he ordered.

The old woman looked right at him and answered, "Well, fine, if that's what you want, but could you hurry and do what you need to do?" She closed her eyes and pretended to go back to sleep.

The ghost was surprised that the old woman didn't appear to be at all afraid of him. Through lowered lashes, she watched him move toward the window. He was tall and thin and wore a nightcap and old slippers. His clothes looked old and worn, and there was dust all over his head and shoulders. The ghost wailed and moaned and tore at the windowsill with his long, boney fingers.

As quick as thought he was back at her bedside. "Go back to sleep and see nothing," he hissed. She could almost feel his boney hands on her throat. As soon as he moved back to the window, she peeked out from under the covers and watched him as he took tools from his coat pockets and began to pry at the wood beneath the windowsill. Suddenly the wood gave way and a torrent of gold coins began to flow onto the floor. The ghost laughed and pulled the gold from the hollow place beneath the window and began to stack the gold pieces up in neat piles and count them with relish. At the last stroke of midnight, he threw the coins back into their hiding place and replaced the wood around the window.

The old woman wondered if she had dreamed the whole thing. She lay awake listening to the rain and waiting for the dawn. As soon as it was light, she dressed and left the room. She saw a maid in the hall.

"Did you see a ghost last night, mistress?" the girl asked.

"Indeed, I did. Please go and tell your master to come quickly to my room."

Soon the entire family was there in her room and she told them all about the strange occurrences. When she came to the part in her story about the gold, they could not believe her.

"Go and look for yourselves," she insisted.

Tools were sent for and the wood was pried off the space beneath the window. When the gold began to flow out of the hole in the wall it seemed to go on and on as if it would never stop. Finally, the floor was covered in gold coins and the family and servants stood there in amazement.

"Where did this money come from?" asked their guest.

The grandfather was the only one who could answer. "A long time ago a miser lived in this house. He was a mean and selfish man who had not a friend in the world. He scorned the poor and was a cruel master to his servants. He would do anything to accumulate more wealth."

"When he died there was no one to mourn him or say a good word about him. Not a single piece of his gold was found and so he was buried in a pauper's grave, with no stone above nor a flower to console him. Although many people looked for it, no one ever found this hiding place. Who would have ever thought that his treasure was hidden under the windowsill?"

"I believe the poor man's ghost came back to this room, night after night, to count his money, making noise so that someone would find it and relieved him of his burden. I doubt that his ghost will ever bother us again."

"Well," said the rain lady. "If this is true, and I was able to give a soul a little rest, then I am happy."

Hearing these words, the gentleman continued. "Please, kind woman, stay another night with us and all the nights to come. We can use someone like you as a member of our household."

"No, thank you kind sir," she replied with a smile. "I must continue my journey."

And though the family begged, the old woman refused to stay. When she left, it was still raining, but she was warmed by the kind words of her grateful hosts and the gift of gold that lay in her bag.

One of many stories about travelers who de-ghost the haunted house—the original ghost busters! A version can be found in Adele de Leeuw's book Legends and Folk Tales of Holland.

The Lord of Death

India

Once, a long time ago, there was a road. Legend had it, that anyone who traveled along this road soon died.

One day a very old man happened to be walking along this road and decided to rest from his travels. He sat down on a stone beneath a tree. Suddenly, he saw a scorpion scurry out from beneath a nearby stone and, as he watched, the scorpion turned into an enormous snake and glided down the road. The old man was so amazed that he stood up and followed the snake as it slithered along, determined to find out all he could about the strange creature.

The snake traveled down the road, day and night, shadowed by the old man.

Once it crawled into an inn and killed several travelers. Another time it went into a palace and killed the king and his youngest daughter. Wherever the snake passed, the weeping and wailing of those left grieving were its legacy. For days and days, weeks and months, the old man quietly followed the snake in wonder.

Finally, the road ended at a broad and swift river. On the banks of this river were some people who had journeyed far and needed to cross the river but had no money for the ferry. The snake now turned into a water buffalo and slowly approached the river. When the travelers sitting by its banks saw the buffalo, they thought that it was going to swim across and so some of them sat on its broad back as it began to swim the river while others took hold of its tail. As soon as the beast was in the middle of the river it began to buck and kick. All the people who were riding the beast fell off and all the people holding its tail lost their grip. Everyone drowned. As this happened, the old man watched it all from a boat he was using to cross the river.

Once the water buffalo reached the other side of the river, it changed into an ox and slowly began to walk along the path that followed the river. A peasant farmer saw the ox and greedily took the animal home and locked him into the pen where he kept his cattle and goats. When nightfall came the ox turned back into a snake and bit each animal, killing them all. Then the snake slithered into the cottage and killed all the members of the peasant's family, leaving him alone to weep and mourn.

The next day, the man followed the snake to another river where it turned into a beautiful young woman, dressed in silks and adorned with beautiful and expensive jewels. This woman stood quietly next to the river's bank until two brothers, returning from the wars, approached her. At that moment, she began to weep.

"What is the matter and why are you crying?" they asked.

"My husband was bending down to take a drink when he fell into the river and drowned. I am alone. I have no family and I have no friends. What will I do?"

The oldest brother, overcome by her beauty, said, "Please, come home with me and be my wife. I will take care of you."

"Alright," said the woman, "but only on one condition. You must never ask me to do any work around the house, and no matter what it is that I want, you must give it to me without any questions."

As soon as the young man had agreed, the woman spoke again, "At the end of this path there is a well. Go and bring me some fresh water to drink. Your younger brother can stay with me while you are gone."

When the older brother was out of sight, the beautiful woman turned and spoke to the younger brother. "You are the one I really wanted. I merely said those things to get rid of your brother. Run away with me now and I will be yours."

"Never," cried the young man. "You are my brother's promised wife and I will treat you like a sister and nothing more or less."

When the older brother returned the young woman began to weep and cry. "While you were gone your younger brother begged me run away with him. He is a villain."

Without thinking, the older brother angrily drew his sword and attacked the younger, who struggled to defend himself. They fought long and hard, and finally they both died, each one at the end of the other's sword. In an instant, the girl took the form of the snake and slithered down the river path. Once more, the old man followed as silently as a shadow, watching and wondering. Finally, the snake turned into an old man, bent with age, leaning on a walking stick. When the old man saw the snake change into someone very much like himself, he summoned his courage and approached the other man.

"Who are you and what is your business in this world?" he asked.

The old man, who had been a snake and so many other creatures, smiled. "I am the Lord of Death. It is my charge to travel and bring death to this world."

The old man who had followed the Lord of Death paused. "Can you take me now?" he asked, "for I am weary of my travels and my heart is sad after watching you bring so much misery into this world."

The Lord of Death slowly shook his head "It is not your time. I can only take those whose time has come to an end. You have many years to live, but I will see you again." With that the Lord of Death vanished.

This is an amazing story that puts death into a very real and stark perspective. A version can be found in Flora Anne Steel's book Tales of the Punjab.

The Gratitude of the Elephant

Vietnam

In Vietnam, when the Le Dynasty lost its empire, an elephant of the royal herd fled to the forest. At that time, elephants were used to lead the troops into battle. This elephant had earned many merits during the war and the king had awarded it with the title of Officer and had three golden rings placed around its neck.

When the Le Dynasty was defeated, the new king, knowing that this elephant was a good fighting elephant, sent many soldiers to find him. But the elephant always ran away. It was believed that he wanted to remain faithful to the old empire.

One day his old keeper, Doi Mau, who had become an old and poor man, went to the forest to collect wood. Upon arriving at a clearing, he heard a loud noise and saw a huge elephant rushing toward him. He was so scared that he fell and lost consciousness. When he came back to his senses, he saw the elephant standing quietly near him, gently touching him with his trunk.

When the elephant saw that the old man had awoken, he cried out in joy. He put the man gently on his back with his trunk and guided the man's hands toward his neck.

Because of the gold rings around the elephant's neck, Doi Mau recognized the old elephant that he had taken care of a long time ago. The two friends were very happy to find each other. The elephant took good care of Doi Mau and brought him food and water.

When evening came, Doi Mau wanted to go home. The elephant brought him to the border of the forest, but also kept taking Doi Mau's hand to his neck. Doi Mau understood that his friend wanted to give him the golden rings. The elephant seemed to know that Doi Mau was poor now and that the golden rings could help. Doi Mau told the elephant that he needed to go home and get the necessary tools to take the rings off. The elephant seemed to understand. He stayed there while Doi Mau went home.

Doi Mau returned with the tools and found the elephant at the same place he had left him. Quickly the rings were removed. The elephant touched the old man gently with his trunk, cried out a few times, as though to say good-bye, and then went back into the forest.

This delightful story of loyalty can be found in the book Legends and Folklore of Viet Nam *by Tam Dang Wei. The story is used with her permission. Tam Dang Wei learned the stories in her book from her parents and her nurse. She wrote the book to share the stories with her own family.*

The Old Soldier and the Magic Sack

Spain (Basque)

A long time ago, when beings from the world of the fairies and those from the world of men often crossed paths, there was an old soldier who had been wounded in a war and now sat begging for alms beneath a wayside cross.

One day, two travelers passed the poor man by as he cried for alms.

"Please, kind sirs, a few coins to ease the hunger of an old soldier no longer fit to fight."

Hearing this, one of the travelers paused. "Well, my friend," he said. "You must make a choice if you want my help. Do you want a seat in heaven when you die or this magic sack that will take care of all your earthly needs?"

The other traveler leaned forward, near the soldier's ear. "Take your seat in heaven," he whispered, but the old soldier would have none of the stranger's advice.

"Easy for you to say, you who have all you need and perhaps all you'll ever need. My family and I are hungry. If I did not have to eat, I would choose Paradise, but I still live here on this earth and would rather have the sack."

The first traveler pulled a bag from inside his coat and handed it to the old soldier. "When you are in need, simply tell the sack, 'I need such and such, Trente-ku-tchilo' and the sack will provide what is needed."

The soldier fell to his knees in thanks, and called his blessings to the men long after they had disappeared down the road. He stood up and hurried toward home to show the newfound magic to his wife and share his good fortune with his family. As he walked along, he passed by the baker's shop just as the man was opening his doors for the day. The aroma of fresh bread spilled out into the streets. This reminded the old man that he had not eaten for a day or more and that he was very hungry.

He called to the baker, "Sir, can you spare a bit of bread for an old soldier who is too tired and worn out to fight for his king?"

"Do you think I work every day so I can support the likes of you?" replied the baker. "If you have no money, then you get no bread. Move on."

"So much for Christian charity," said the soldier, as he reached for the bag that the traveler had given him. "Sack, I need bread, Trente-ku-tchilo," he said. Much to the surprise of the baker and all the people on the street, the soldier then pulled a fine loaf of fresh bread from his sack.

As he walked further, the old soldier passed a tax collector whose donkey was weighted down with bags of gold.

"Please, can you spare a coin or two for an old man who served his king long ago in the wars?"

"Do you think I work from dawn to dusk, collecting taxes, so I can give them to you? Away with you."

"Well, there's another example of charity," said the man. "Sack, I need money, Trente-ku-tchilo." To the surprise of the tax collector, the soldier's sack was immediately filled all the way to the top with gold coins.

When the old soldier reached home he shared his new wealth with all of his family. No longer would they be hungry or cold or poor. A house that once was filled with tears of sorrow now was filled with tears of joy.

One day, sometime later, the soldier returned home from his daily walk to find his wife in tears, shaking with fear.

"What is the matter? Are you or one of the children ill?"

"Husband, every time you go away, an ogre comes to the house. He peers through the window and rattles the door latch, trying to get in. I am sure that some day he will find his way in and do me and the children terrible harm."

The next day the soldier pretended to go for a walk but returned along the hedge and hid near the kitchen door. When the monster appeared, he said to his sack, "Sack, I need this monster, Trente-ku-tchilo." The sack stretched and the ogre was drawn into it. The soldier killed the creature and rid his family and the surrounding villages of the menace.

After that, they lived in peace, but, from time to time, the old soldier worried about the choice he made all those years ago when he accepted the sack from the traveler. "What will happen to me when I die and must travel to the other world?" he thought. "Where will I go once I'm dead?" He made his wife promise him that when he finally met death, she would tie his sack around his wrist and place it in the coffin with him.

At long last death came for old soldier as it does for us all. His wife kept her promise and the sack was with him as he journeyed to the other side. He walked and walked, until he finally came to the gates of Paradise.

The old soldier knocked upon the gate for a long time. Finally, the gate keeper opened it just a crack and the old man could see that the gatekeeper was none other than the man who had given him the sack, the man who had given him a choice.

"Old soldier, you made your choice long ago, my friend. You must leave and never return."

Just as the gatekeeper was about to shut the gate, the soldier said, "Sack, I need this gatekeeper, Trente-ku-tchilo." In that instant the gatekeeper found himself inside the sack and the string pulled tight.

At first the gatekeeper demanded to be freed and then he pleaded to be let out, but the old soldier was firm.

"As soon as you let me into Paradise then I will let you out, but not a minute before."

The gatekeeper knew there was no other way and so the old soldier entered Paradise. Now, I think the gatekeeper was just a little pleased to see that the soldier had made the right choice and used his sack so well, don't you?

_____

Magic sacks and deals with the heavenly gatekeeper and getting the best of the tax collector make this well-known story unique and fun. You can find a version in Tales of a Basque Grandmother *by Francis Carpenter.*

The Crane's Purse

Russia

Once, not so long ago, a poor old man and woman who lived in a rundown shack and had little to eat, happened to find some barley seeds. With great care they planted them at the edge of their little garden.

After a week had passed, the old man noticed the barley had grown to the height of his knee. He called for his wife and they laughed over the prospect of a nice crop of barley to keep them through the bitter winter. The next day, the barley had grown up to the old man's waist. He ran to his wife who was overjoyed at their good luck in finding such wonderful seeds.

On the very next day, the old man went out to his patch of barley only to find an enormous bird, a crane, standing in the middle of his small plot, eating away at the barley.

Even worse, the barley was trampled down where the great bird had walked.

The old man ran back to his shack. "Wife, a great crane has landed in our barley patch and trampled it down."

"Is the bird still there?" she asked.

"Yes, he is, curse him."

"You still have your old gun. Go out and kill the intruder or we'll have nothing left to see us through the winter."

The old man loaded his ancient musket and, quickly and silently, went back to his barley. The crane was still there, so the man crept closer and closer, raised his gun, and fired.

But, when the smoke cleared, there was no crane. Instead, there was a tall handsome gentleman standing where the crane had been. You see, the crane was no bird at all, but a wizard in disguise.

"Good morning, my fine old friend. Are you trying to shoot me? Is this your barley patch I'm standing in?" The gentleman seemed somewhat amused.

The little old man was shocked to see the man standing in the very place where only a moment before the crane had stood. "Yes sir, it is my barley."

"What would you like to have for your barley crop?" the gentleman asked.

"What ever your lordship would chose to give me," replied the old man, timidly.

"Follow the green path through the silken grass, and there you will find a great castle. Walk up the steps, and there the guard will ask you who you are seeking. Tell him that you seek the crane and he will let you in." With that, the wizard spread his arms and they turned into wings, and he flew away, across the tops of the trees and out of sight.

The old man watched as if in a dream. He rubbed his eyes and wondered if what he thought had happened had truly happened. He stared across his little plot of barley and saw a green path where no path had been the day before. The path wound its way through silken grass.

The old man left his musket on the ground and followed the path. It wove its way through the forest, and soon the old man was getting tired. Just when he thought he might sit down for a little rest, the path opened up onto a field and, sitting in the middle of that field, there was a castle as rich as that of any king. The old man walked up the steps and a guard stepped forward. "Who do you seek, old man?"

"I seek the crane," said the old man.

The doors of the castle opened, and the crane wizard was standing there waiting for the old man. The lord of the castle led him through room after room, each one more magnificent than the other.

They finally came to a room where a table was spread with food and drink. His host told the old man to eat and drink his fill. Without having to be told twice, he ate and drank as never before. When the old man was finished, the wizard smiled and asked, "Now what price do you ask of me for your barley?"

The old man was still overwhelmed by the magic of the day. "Give me what you think is fair," he replied.

The crane wizard walked into another room and came back with a small silken purse. He handed it to the old man and said, "This purse will provide you with food whenever you ask. Just say the words, 'Little purse, give to me food and drink.' When you do this, tables and chairs and whatever you need for your feast will be provided. When you are finished eating and drinking, just say, 'Food, drink, table, chair, go back into the purse.' Every thing will disappear into the purse until next time you need it. Now, take this magic purse and be on your way."

The old man took the purse and bowed to his host, but when he straightened himself, the room, the castle, and his host were all gone and he stood back on that green path with the silken grass.

Eager to share a magical meal with his wife, the old man set off at a lively pace for home. Along the way, though, he began to feel weary and thought that a little snack might prove refreshing. "Little purse, give to me food and drink," he said. In an instant the forest had changed into a beautiful, shining room, with a golden chair and an ivory table, spread with a feast. The old man ate and drank as he had before and then he said, "Food, drink, table, chair, go back into the purse." This time he was no longer standing in the forest where he had been but was standing right outside his old cottage door.

He walked into his home laughing like a schoolboy. "Good day, wife," he called out.

"Husband," she cried, "I was worried that the wolves had taken you or that you were lost in the woods. Are you well?"

"Never better," he said. " Sit down and listen to my story." His wife sat down and the old man told her everything. He told her of the crane changing into a wizard, the path through the forest to the castle, and, finally, the magic purse. "Are you hungry, dear one?" he asked.

"I've been so worried about you that I have had little time to think about eating. Besides, there is little in the house to satisfy us."

The husband laughed again and said, "Little purse, give to me food and drink."

The room changed into a beautiful, shining banquet hall, with golden chairs and the same ivory table groaning under the weight of a feast. The old woman clapped her hands and laughed out loud. "You have been to another world and look what you have brought us!"

From that day on, the old couple dined well and started to grow plump and healthy. Their neighbors thought this odd, since they were too old to work and still lived in the same run down cottage. Rumors spread, until the rumors reached the ears of the duke, the ruler of the kingdom, a greedy and harsh man. When he heard of the old couple's change, he thought that perhaps they had found a treasure and if this was so, then he needed to increase their rent.

The duke rode out to see the couple. He found the old man sitting in front of his run-down cottage, whistling a happy tune.

"Good day to you, old man."

"Good day to you, my lord."

"How are you and your wife?"

"We are well, my lord. In fact, we are better than well. Would you care to join us for a meal?"

The duke took one look at the cottage with its leaking roof and sagging walls and imagined what it must be like on the inside. "Perhaps we could dine out here, old man?"

"You will be surprised, my lord, at the difference between the outside and the inside of my cottage."

The duke walked into the cottage just as the old man spoke to his purse, "Little purse, give to me food and drink." The room changed into that beautiful dining hall and the duke was truly amazed. He ate and drank well, for he was not a man to pass up a free meal. After he had eaten his fill, he grew more envious by the minute and wanted that purse more than anything.

"Old man, it is not right that you should set a table that is better than mine. Let us make a bargain. If you will give me the purse, I will provide you with all you need. Meat and drink, barley and wine, butter and bread. I shall send you a cow and a pig and two servants to wait upon you. I might even fix up this old cottage. What do you say?"

The last thing the old man wanted was to give up his purse, but he was afraid of the duke. He went to ask his wife, who was awed by the duke and had chosen to stay in the yard. She had her ear to the door, though, and had heard it all.

"Well, wife, what do you think?"

"I think that if we do not give him the purse he will take it anyway and then we will be left with nothing. At least, he will provide us with something if we agree to his offer."

The old man agreed, and so the bargain was made and the duke rode away with the silken purse. He sent the old couple all he had promised—food, wine, animals, and servants. The old couple lived at ease, while the duke entertained with the magic purse, becoming the envy of all his noble friends.

All went well, for a time. Then, one day, when the provisions the duke had sent were almost gone, the old man sent the maid to the duke's castle to ask for more. The duke was very put out by the girl's request. "What do they do all day, those two old folks? Haven't I given them enough? In fact, I've given them far too much. They need to work and if they can't work they should beg." He sent the girl back to the couple with nothing. She told them the news and they were shocked. The maid and the manservant both left, returning to the castle with the cow and the pig.

Poor once again, the old couple could not believe their bad luck. "What shall we do?" asked the wife.

"I will go to the crane wizard and tell him that we lost the purse. Perhaps, he will take pity on us and give us another one."

"If you tell him that, you will be lying."

"Better to lie than to starve to death," replied her husband.

The old man walked into the woods and found the green path that wound its way through the silken grass. He followed the path for a long time, longer it seemed than the first time he walked it. Finally, when he was too tired to take another step, he came to the castle. He walked up the steps and the guard at the door stopped him and said, "Whom do you seek?"

"I seek the crane," answered the man.

The doors opened and the crane wizard was waiting inside. "My dear old friend," said the great bird, "welcome."

The crane wizard led the old man through several rooms as splendid as the old man could imagine until they came to a banquet hall set with a feast. "Sit down, my dear little old one and eat and drink your fill."

The old man hesitated, and the crane wizard asked, "What is the problem, my friend? Has someone done you wrong?"

The old man looked at his host and replied, "I wanted to tell you that we had lost the magic purse, but that would have been a lie. In truth, the duke has taken it away from us." He told the crane wizard the whole story.

"You must be hungry and thirsty, my friend. Sit down here, at the table, and enjoy yourself." The old man sat but instead of eating he wept.

"My lord, could you please give us another purse so we will not go hungry?"

"No, my little friend," the crane wizard shook his head. " I cannot give you another purse like that one, but I will give you something."

The wizard went into the next room and came back with a large velvet bag, tied tightly with silken cord. "Take this bag home with you. Send your wife off to the duke and have her tell him that now you have a much larger purse. Let her invite him to come and see it for himself. When he walks through your door, untie the silken cord and say, 'You twelve heroes climb out and give the duke what he deserves.' When they have given the duke what he deserves say, 'You twelve heroes, stand over there by the threshold.' Then, and only then, do you ask the duke, to return your silken purse."

The old man thanked the crane wizard, and started his journey home. He walked a great distance, it seemed longer than any other time he had walked it, but he never stopped. He walked and walked until finally he came to his own run-down cottage.

The husband told his wife what the wizard had said and all about the new gift he had given them. He also told her about her part in the plan. At first she was frightened, but when she thought of how the duke had treated them, she found her courage.

The old woman went to the duke, telling him the story of the new, larger bag that her husband had received. The duke decided then and there that he had to have this bag too. He ordered his coach and even had the old wife sit beside him on the trip back to her cottage.

Soon they arrived and the duke followed the woman inside.

"Well, my good man," said the duke, "what marvels have you to show me this time?"

The old man smiled and said, "I'm not quite sure, my lord, but we shall see." He untied the silken cord and said, "You twelve heroes climb out of the bag and give the duke what he deserves."

Out of the bag sprang twelve huge warriors with cubs and whips in their hands. They set about the duke, hitting and whipping him until he begged for mercy. Then the man said, "Now, my twelve heroes, go and stand by the threshold."

The poor man turned and spoke to the duke, "Now, my lord, give me back my purse."

"Take care," cried the duke, "or I'll have you hanged for what you just did to me."

The old man was no longer afraid of the duke. "Give me back what is rightfully mine, my lord. You see my twelve heroes all stand by the door. If you do not give it back, then you will receive a beating such that your father, or grandfather, or great grandfather never dreamed of in their long lives."

"The purse is back at my castle under lock and key. Let me go back and I will return with it."

The poor man laughed. "You ask me to trust you, my lord? No, send your coachman instead to retrieve the purse."

The duke called his coachman, who approached with fright when he saw the heroes standing by the door. The magic warriors allowed him entrance. The duke gave the coachman the key to the hiding place where he kept the magic purse. The duke watched the heroes, wondering if he could run past them, but they stood like statues, their clubs and whips held high over their heads.

The coachman returned and put the purse into the old man's hands.

"Now, will you release me?" asked the duke.

"Of course, my lord," said the man. But then he turned to his twelve heroes and said to them, "My heroes, open ranks and let the duke pass by. But again, you must give the duke what he deserves. You know he beats the peasants and gives not a thought to their pain, so let him feel a beating as he passes you and let him know the pain." The heroes whipped and beat the duke as he tried to run back to his coach. Finally, he stumbled into the coach and was off in a cloud of dust.

"Thank you, my twelve heroes. Now into the bag once again." The heroes disappeared into the velvet bag and the old man hung it up on a peg near the door.

Turning to his wife, the old man kissed her and laughed. "Now we need a good meal. Little purse, give me and my lovely wife food and drink." The room changed into the shining banquet hall, with golden chairs, and an ivory table groaning under the weight of the old couple's feast. When they finished eating, they laughed, and sang, and danced around the beautiful hall that filled the inside of their humble cottage. They had their magic purse and they would not go hungry again. They had their twelve heroes and would not live in fear again. And so they lived to the end of their days, as happy as they ever could be.

―――――――――――――――――

This is one of those great tales of gifts and theft, courage and revenge, magic and cunning. The idea of the twelve heroes, living in a sack, hanging on a peg on the wall, seems a wonderful way to discourage anyone from foul deeds. A lovely version can be found in Ruth Manning-Sanders's book, Sir Green Hat and the Wizard.

Chapter Seven

Our Animal Elders

The Beaver Woman and the Eagle

United States

A Lakota/Dakota Story retold by Dovie Thomason
©2006 Dovie Thomason, used with permission.

Long ago, there was an old Beaver Woman working by a stream bed, busily taking down saplings, stripping away their branches and leaves. But she was not so busy that she did not notice a great Eagle circling high above her in the sky. She was not so busy that she did not notice the whistling of the wind through his wings as he flew, diving toward the earth, intending to make her his breakfast.

Quickly, she dove into the water and disappeared. The disappointed Eagle circled closer and landed on the branch of a dead cottonwood, his eyes fixed on the spot where she had disappeared under the water. Suddenly, a brown head, touched with the silver of many seasons, popped up from a different spot in the stream, not where Eagle was glaring intently.

"What gives you the right to attack the grandmother of a gentle and hardworking people?"

The Eagle turned his fierce gaze on her, "I am hungry. I am Eagle."

The old Beaver Woman looked back at him fearlessly. "Yes, but why don't you try to live as ours do? To find value in working hard and leaving others alone to live their lives."

The Eagle scoffed, "That is easy for you to say. Not everyone can fell trees with their teeth—and who would want to be like you? Who would want to live by eating branches, leaves and bark? I am not an old woman; I am a great warrior!"

"Ah," she said, gently, "it seems to be true. Some seem to live just to cause trouble for others. But couldn't you possibly also learn to play fair? To work for a living and do something that would also help others? My work does not benefit just me and my family. I widen the streambeds. I make ponds and therefore make it possible for many others to live. But you—you use *your* power just to terrify those who are weaker and smaller than you. Perhaps there is much you could learn from *my* people."

At this, the Eagle gave her another sharp and hungry look. Before he could move even one feather, the old Beaver Woman turned and, slapping her tail on the water, dove deep to the bottom of the pond.

There, she crawled into her dry lodge of stick and mud and fed her grandchildren and ate a good meal herself. Then they slept, curled safe and comfortable in their lodge within the waters. Above them, on that cottonwood branch, Eagle waited and waited and watched the fading ripples in the water. The winds whistled and rattled the dead branches where he clung. The waters became frosted with a crust of ice.

And, though he was scornful of the old Beaver Woman's simple ways and still full of pride about who he thought he was, that day it was the Eagle who went hungry while the old Beaver Woman was warm and well fed.

A story that illustrates how the proud can be brought to an understanding of others. Thanks to Dovie Thomason for this tale from the Lakota/Dakota people.

The Bremen Town Musicians

Germany

Once a long time ago there was a man who farmed his land with his donkey. The donkey plowed the fields, pulled the reaper, helped drag stones from the field to make the wall around the farm, and hauled the fruits of his labor to market. But, as time would have it and, as always, time wins in the end, the donkey began to grow old and couldn't work around the farm any more. The farmer purchased a new animal and treated his old friend as an honored guest. He slept late in his stall, ate the best grain, and had the run of the farm like a pet. He would often get into the vegetable patch, angering the farmer's wife, or get tangled in the laundry that hung outside on the line across the barnyard, causing her to scream.

One day the donkey was happily eating some flowers under the window of the kitchen when he heard the farmer and his wife talking. They were talking about him.

"That old donkey is good for nothing. All he does is sleep and eat, eat and sleep. This is a farm and an animal has to be useful. A donkey should be working and pulling his weight on a farm," said the wife.

"That donkey worked side by side with me for many years and he deserves a rest. He's as much a friend as any man I know," countered the farmer.

"Well, I don't care. He's too old. I'm going to sell him. Maybe I can get a few coins from the glue factory." The wife sounded very serious.

The old donkey thought to himself, "I've worked hard and now I'm off to the glue factory. Oh, no. I'm off to see the world. I'm leaving this farm." With tears in his eyes the old donkey raised the latch on the gate and walked out into the country lane that ran beside the farm. Now, he had heard of a place called Bremen Town from the horse of a traveling salesman. The horse told him that the people of that town liked music so much that all you had to do was stand and sing on the corner of any street and people would throw golden coins at your feet. The donkey thought to himself that Bremen Town sounded like paradise.

"I'm a good singer," he said to himself and then proceeded to sing, "Hee haw, hee haw, hee haw." He thought he sounded beautiful.

As the donkey walked down the road he came to the next farm and saw a goat sitting sadly outside the gate.

"Afternoon, neighbor," said the donkey. "Why the long face?"

"My master says that I'm too old to be of any use," said the goat. "He's taking me to the butcher to be made into sausages."

"That's terrible," said the donkey. Then an idea came to him. "Can you sing?"

"Sure," replied the goat, who proceeded to sing, "Bleattttt, bleattttt, bleattttt."

"That's beautiful," said the donkey. "Come with me to Bremen Town and we'll become a duet. We'll sing in the streets and the people will shower us with gold." And so it was. The two old animals continued down the road.

They walked until they came to the next farm and there was an old black dog, crying next to the gate.

"Hello, neighbor. Why the tears?" said the donkey.

"My master says I'm too old to hunt, so now he has a new hunting dog. They don't want me around. I heard them say they're going to shoot me." The old dog started crying again, tears flowing down his face.

The donkey knew right away what to say. "That's terrible, but can you sing?"

The dog looked up. "I think so. Arf-arf-arf-arf-arf-ahooo," he said.

"That's beautiful," said the donkey. "Come with us. We'll be a trio and we'll sing in the streets of Bremen Town and earn a fortune." The dog agreed and so the three new friends took off down the road.

They walked and talked until they came to the next farm. And there was an old tomcat sitting on the fence, moaning and weeping.

"Afternoon, neighbor. What's the problem?" said the three.

The cat looked at them and said, "I'm not as fast as I used to be and I don't catch mice like I used to, so my mistress got a new cat. She says she's going to put me in a sack and drown me in the river."

"That's terrible," said the dog. "Can you sing?"

"Of course," said the cat. "Meow, meow, meow, meooooowwww."

"That's beautiful," said the donkey. "Come with us and we'll become a quartet and sing all over Bremen Town and make our fortune." The cat agreed and the four new friends headed down the road on their way to Bremen Town.

They walked and talked and sang until they came to the last farm before the woods. There, sitting on the gate, was an old rooster, his head down, crying softly to himself.

"Hello, neighbor. Why the sorrow?" said the donkey.

The rooster looked up and said, "Every day, for years, I have announced the rising of the sun to wake the farmer and his wife, but now I'm old and sometimes

I sleep late. The wife says that she's getting a new rooster and that they're having me for Sunday dinner."

"That's terrible," said the donkey. "Can you sing?"

"Of course I can," said the rooster. "Cock a doodle do, cock a doodle do."

"That's beautiful. Come with us and we'll become a quintet and amaze the people of Bremen Town with our harmonies. We'll make a fortune."

And so the five new friends walked down the road and soon came to the edge of the forest. Now, the forest was dark and deep and very frightening to these five farm animals. As they made their way among the tall trees they walked closer and closer to each other. The night sounds seemed louder in the forest than they did on the farm.

Finally, the rooster said, "I'll fly up to a branch and see if I can see a trail or a cabin or some sign of people."

He was only gone a minute before he fluttered back down. "There is a very narrow trail that ends in a small clearing, and in the middle of the clearing there's a house with smoke coming out of the chimney."

"I think we should all go there and sing them a song. I'm sure they'll give us a wonderful supper in exchange for our music," said the donkey.

With rooster in the lead, they all walked down the path. When they got to the clearing they stopped.

"I'll go first and have a look around. I'm used to people and their houses," said the dog.

He walked over to the house and stretched up to look in the window. He studied the inside, looking left and right, and soon was back with his friends.

"I think that these men might be robbers. There are piles of silver in one corner and gold in the other. The table is filled with food." As he named the foods each animal heard a favorite and grew more and more hungry.

Goat said, "I think we should just step through the door and surprise them. We'll all go in, shoulder-to-shoulder, singing in our best voices. They'll love it."

"Won't work," said the dog. "It's a human door, only wide enough for one or two of us at a time."

"Wait," said cat. "If goat climbs on donkey's back and dog on goat's back, and I get on dog's back and rooster stands on donkey's head, we could all get through the door at once." Everyone agreed it was a great idea and soon they were all in place for the performance. Donkey quietly walked onto the porch and suddenly kicked the door open. All the animals started singing at the same time. "Hee haw, hee haw, bleattttt, arf, arf, meoooowww, cock a doodle dooooooo!!!"

The robbers stood up stared at the sight in the doorway, and headed for the back door, screaming, and off they ran, into the woods.

The friends waited quite a while for their audience to return, but, after what seemed like a long time they just decided to have supper without them. After they had eaten most of the food on the table, they grew tired and decided to spend the night in the cabin. Donkey slept on the front porch, goat behind the door, dog under the table, just in case anything dropped on the floor, cat slept near the fireplace so he could stay warm near the hot coals, and rooster perched on top of the cabin, near the chimney.

Meanwhile, the robbers were out in the woods cold and hungry.

Their leader turned to them. "Did you see that monster? What an awful roar it had? What do you think it was?"

"It looked like a donkey with a goat on its back."

"No, it was a dog sitting on a goat."

"I think it was a cat perched on a dog."

"Looked to me like a rooster riding a donkey."

"Wait, one of us has to go back and find out what it is. How else will we ever get our money back?" They all looked at the youngest thief. "You go."

"Me?" he cried.

"You," the rest chorused.

The young thief crept back to the cabin. By now it was dark, not even a star to light his way. He quietly crept through the back door. He walked past the sleeping dog and decided to blow on the embers in the fireplace and rekindle the fire so he could see. When he did this, a spark hit the cat's tail. The cat woke up and scratched the robber's face. He backed into the table and the dog bit him in the leg as he staggered to the door, the goat put his head down and rammed him with his horns. When he stumbled out the front door, the donkey woke and kicked him through the air and half way across the clearing. All the while the rooster kept crowing, "Coo coo careee."

Battered and bitten, the young thief made his way back to his friends. "Well," asked the leader, "What's going on?"

"Its horrible," said the young man. "First a witch was sitting in the fireplace and she scratched me. Then a troll came out from under the table and bit me. At the front door a demon poked me with his horns. When I made it to the porch a giant kicked me half way to the moon. All the while a wicked wizard kept screaming, "Bring him to me." It was a nightmare. The thieves turned and ran and didn't stop until dawn.

The next day, the five friends decided that they liked the cabin, and since their audience never returned, they made it their home. They never got to Bremen Town but they were happy and started each day with a song.

_____

Old animals also have their own brand of wisdom. My old dog Jack teaches me something new everyday about growing old gracefully and, at the same time, kicking and fighting to keep a bit of youth in my life. This is a common story and easy to find. Read the unusual version from Finland, found in Dragons, Ogres, & Wicked Witches *by Milos Maly where the animals battle the devil instead of robbers.*

The Lion's Share

Ethiopia

L ong ago, there lived an old hyena and his nine sons. Although the father was still in good health, he liked to stay in his den while the sons went out to hunt. The father told his sons that he was staying behind to guard their home, but really, he was getting just a little lazy. Late at night, after they had eaten what the sons brought back to the den, he told his sons stories about his younger days when he hunted and fought and was fearless. He made each one understand that he expected them to follow in his footsteps as a hunter and a warrior.

One evening, the nine young hyenas went out hunting. They had not gone far when they were joined by a great lion who lived nearby. The hyenas were about to fade away into the shadows when the lion stopped them.

"Listen, neighbors," he said. "Why don't we hunt together tonight? I've been searching for two hours and have found nothing. With your sense of smell and my size and strength we might get a good meal yet tonight. If we do, we'll each get a good share of our catch."

The nine brothers didn't want to hunt with the lion but they were so afraid of him that they went along with his idea. Luck was with them almost right away. Their keen noses led them to a tree where a hunter had put his day's catch high in the branches, suspended by a rope so he could retrieve it the next day. Now, it was too high for the hyenas to reach but not for the lion. The lion stretched his great body up and tore the hunter's bag from the rope. As it fell to the ground, ten guinea hens spilled out.

"You see the wisdom of hunting together," said the lion. "Now, we can share the food."

The lion took the nine fattest hens for himself and gave the hyenas the small, scrawny tenth bird. The hyenas howled their disapproval.

"What's the problem?" asked the lion, threateningly. "Didn't I divide them fairly?"

The hyenas were too afraid to answer. The lion picked up his nine hens and walked over to eat them under the sprawling canopy of a nearby tree. The nine brothers knew their father would be angry if they failed to bring him anything, so they took the last hen and returned to their den.

The father was furious that they brought home so little. "How can I keep up my strength if the only thing you bring me is a bag of bones and feathers?"

"Father," said the oldest son, "we had planned a very fine dinner for you but we didn't realize how big the lion's share would be." They told their father the story of hunting with the lion and how he had divided the food.

The old hyena howled with rage. He called his children cowards and weaklings. He was so angry, the sons were afraid that he would explode with rage.

At last, he was so beside himself, he picked up the tenth guinea hen and strode out of the den. "Follow me and I will show you how to handle a lion. We will exchange this insult for our fair share. You are so lucky that I am your father and that courage still runs in my veins."

As they came near to the lion's tree, the old hyena called out, "Lion! I need to talk to you."

There was a long silence, followed by what seemed to be a yawn. The lion had obviously been sleeping off his feast. Then came a great roar and, slowly, the lion stood and looked down at the old hyena. The big cat's mane seemed to glow in the moonlight and his teeth shone like jewels. He was the very picture of power and strength.

"Well, friend hyena," he purred softly, "what is it you want from me this night?"

The old hyena looked up at that huge beast and felt very small. Swallowing hard and clearing his throat, he said, "Well, my friend, my sons told me how generous you were when you shared your food with them, so we have come to present you with the last hen."

Pushing the bird toward the lion with his paw, the old hyena bowed low and slowly backed away and then he and his sons crept back to the safety of their den.

Part of wisdom is knowing when to fight and when to give back the tenth hen. Not all elders are heroes, but wisdom often compensates for valor. You can find a version in The Lion's Whiskers & Other Ethiopian Tales *by Brent Ashabranner and Russell Davis.*

The Old Man of Teutli

Mexico

One day a small rabbit ran alone through the countryside. He had no family and was all by himself in the world. As he ran, his stomach started to growl, demanding food.

"Quiet, stomach. There's nothing to eat around here. The harvest has been taken in and the land is dry and parched."

The rabbit ran on, and soon his stomach was growling and gurgling again, but this time for water.

"Quiet down, in there," he said. "I'll look for a cactus or some other plant that may have some moisture, but there are no rivers or creeks or ponds in this dry place."

While he was running along, the small rabbit met an old man wearing a big flat hat. He was so old that he had to lean on a crutch as he walked. His hair was long and white, as was his beard. The rabbit knew at once, as all animals always know these things, that this was the great wise Old Man of Teutli.

The little rabbit ran up to the old man and knelt before him and kissed the ground.

"Old Man of Teutli, my father," cried the rabbit, "where are you going? You should be at home and not walking in this cold night air. Please, go home. If we lose you who will rule us, who will take care of us and guide us?"

The old man smiled and looked down at the small rabbit. "My little friend, everything has dried up. I left my home because I was so cold. I am looking for the sun and its warmth, and, for the people who live in the far mountains. But night is coming on and it's getting colder, and I feel tired and unsteady."

"Father, maybe you are ill or hungry. You should go home and not be out wandering around in the cold of this barren countryside," cried the small rabbit.

"No, my dear little friend, I am fine."

"I know why you are unsteady and tired. You are thirsty. Here, wise man, take this knife and open me up and drink my blood and you will feel better. You will be strong again and able to travel. You will feel the warmth of the sun on your back again."

"My little son," replied the Old Man of Teutli, "I am old and have lived a long life; it will not matter if I should die. But you, little one, are young and have only walked this beautiful world for a short time."

"My dear old father, you have always looked out for me. Your kindness has given me food to eat and water to drink. You have always been a friend to the animals. You must not die, old one. This land is so dry, and so cold, please do as I say. Please drink my blood and save yourself."

"I thank you, my friend, but I know where there are some cacti. I will get some and break them open and drink the juice inside. Then, I promise, I will go home and rest."

"But you, my little rabbit, you run down to Mexcalco and there you will find a cave. Go into the cave and there you will find a crystal-clear spring of water, fresh fruits, and the warmth of summer days. Whatever you need you will find there. Eat well and drink deeply, for I value your good heart."

The small rabbit thanked the old man and once again knelt and kissed the ground in front of him before running toward the cave.

The wise Old Man of Teutli straightened up and threw away his walking stick, and spoke as he watched the little rabbit disappear.

"My little friend, you will never know how I tested your love for me today. My little son, your heart is so much larger, your love, so much deeper than even mine. You have shamed me, little one, and I am richer for it."

Then, the wise Old Man of Teutli walked on.

This sweet little story from Mexico dates back to pre-Spanish days and talks about the rabbit and his devotion to the Old Wise Man. There is a beautiful version in a little book called The Merry Frogs by Idella Purnell.

The Trap

Cameroon

Once, in the days when animals could talk and people listened, there was a drought. The land was dry, the days were hot, and Leopard grew very hungry. All the big animals had gone to the watering hole, and he couldn't lure them away. All the little animals had gone to the tops of the trees to catch a breeze, and he was too big to go up there.

One very hot day, Leopard walked along the jungle floor looking up to see if a monkey or a squirrel might be coming down for a drink so he could have his supper. He never saw the trap. It was a deep pit dug into the earth. With a snap, he fell into the trap. He tried to use his powerful legs to jump out, but the pit was too deep. With his sharp claws, he tried to climb out, but it was too steep. He knew that when the hunters returned they would kill him.

Suddenly, Leopard looked up and saw a small face looking down at him. It was a squirrel.

"Brother Squirrel, won't you help me out of this trap?"

"No," said Squirrel.

"But the hunters will kill me when they return," moaned Leopard.

"Good," cried Squirrel. "You leopards are always chasing and eating us squirrels. Now you'll know what it feels like."

The big cat thought for a moment. "Squirrel, if you help me I'll be your friend. With me as your friend, who would ever pick on you again?"

Squirrel thought for a moment. Everybody picked on him. He looked down at that huge black cat and knew that if it was his friend, no one would ever bully him again.

"Alright. I'll help." Squirrel climbed a tree next to the trap and, as he walked out on a branch that hung over the deep pit, the branch started to bend further and further down until Leopard could reach up and pull himself out. Then, sitting next to each other at the edge of the trap, Leopard and Squirrel talked.

"Squirrel, you saved my life."

"It's great to have a big, strong friend like you."

But Leopard started to remember why he had fallen into the trap. He remembered how hungry he was and how he had been looking for a meal when he fell into the pit. He looked down at that small, fat, juicy squirrel and, quick as a thought, he grabbed the little animal with his huge paw.

"And now Squirrel, I'm going to eat you."

"Eat me? But I saved your life. You promised to be my friend and protect me."

"I know, but the jungle law is that the strong survive and the weak perish. I'm strong, you're weak, so I'm going to eat you."

Squirrel started to squirm and yell as loudly as he could. Suddenly, down the path came Old Man Goat, the wisest animal in the jungle. You could tell he was wise because his beard was long and white.

"What are you two arguing about?" said Goat.

"Leopard is going to eat me."

"What else is new," said Goat.

"You don't understand. I saved his life and he promised to be my friend." Squirrel told Goat the whole story. Goat didn't like the ending. He started to laugh.

Leopard growled, "What are you laughing at, Goat?"

"You," said Goat. "You're trying to play a trick on me. You're trying to make me believe that this puny, little squirrel saved the life of a big, strong cat."

"It's true," they both declared loudly.

"I don't believe you. If it really happened, the way you said it did show me. Do it again, so I can see with my own eyes."

Leopard let go of Squirrel who quickly climbed the tree. Then the leopard jumped to the bottom of the pit.

Goat walked over and spoke to Squirrel. "You come with me, Squirrel," he said. "Leave Leopard where he belongs."

That's what they did and we all know what happened to Leopard when the hunters returned.

_____

This story is found in many cultures, from India to the American South, and the result is always the same. Often one of the characters is human, but I like the interplay between the three animals. There is an excellent version in Tortoise the Trickster *by Lorerto Todd.*

The Monkey and the Boar

Japan

In the old days, there was a musician who traveled from village to village playing music and entertaining the people. In cold weather he would sit inside the inn at which he was staying and play music for other travelers who sat near the fire. On warm days he played outside, where people could hear his samisen and listen to his songs as they passed by. People would throw a few coins into his hat or pay for his meal. It was a hard way to make a living but the man was happy.

One day, he was walking through the mountains during first light and came upon a small baby snow monkey shivering in the frosty air. The man looked around, but there was no other monkey nearby so he assumed the baby monkey was an orphan. He carefully wrapped it up into the folds of his coat and carried it home to his wife. The couple named the little monkey Taro and cared for him like a child. Soon he was growing and getting stronger. Now, Taro was very smart and soon he understood almost everything the musician and his wife said to him. Unfortunately, they never learned to understand him.

One afternoon, when the musician was practicing, Taro started to hop around and sway with the music. Soon, he learned to dance and do somersaults and cartwheels while the man played his samisen. It wasn't long before Taro started to accompany the musician to the villages where he regularly entertained. While the people liked the musician's playing and singing, they loved little Taro. They always shouted for more, clapping and laughing while Taro flew through the air in time to the music. Far more coins found their way into the hat because of Taro's wonderful dancing than the musician's performance.

After many years, the musician and his wife had a child, a little boy they named Bokuden. Now, Bokuden was like all babies—he cried. He soon learned that the louder he cried, the faster his mother and father would come running.

They would look helpless and then, finally turn to Taro and say, "Please, do something." So the little snow monkey would do a somersault or a cartwheel and make funny faces till Bokuden stopped his crying and started to laugh.

Of course, this meant that now poor Taro was working twice as hard, dancing in the villages by day and entertaining the baby by night. The poor monkey was worn out and felt weak all the time. He wasn't young any more and was getting a bit grey around his muzzle. At first, he started to miss a turn or a cartwheel once in a while, but then it happened more and more often, and people gave less and less for the music and dancing. At last, as Taro fell more and more often during the shows, people just walked away, shaking their heads, their coins still in their pockets.

One night, after a very bad day, Taro heard the musician talking to his wife.

"Poor old Taro. He just can't keep up any more. He's getting old and its time for him to retire."

"If he retires what will we do with him?" asked the wife.

"I'll take him back to the mountains where I found him. Perhaps I can find a younger monkey to train and take his place."

Taro heard the whole conversation while he was lying on his bed on the porch. He wanted to tell them that they were his family and that he wanted to stay with them, but they couldn't understand him. Taro was in trouble and he needed advice from someone who was much wiser.

Taro knew who he had to find, the old boar of the forest. Now, everyone knew that the boar was the wisest of all the animals and Taro thought that if anyone could help him it would be the boar.

Taro waited until it got very dark and he heard the sound of snoring from inside the house. He ran down the path, through the gate, and into the woods. He ran until he couldn't run anymore, and that's when he heard a sound and he knew he was not alone. There, in the moonlight, was an enormous old boar. His belly sagged and his tusks were yellow. The bristles on his back were covered in pine needles and he was rooting around looking for mushrooms and other things to eat. He stopped and looked up at Taro with little red eyes that seemed like hot coals in the night.

"What do you want here?" asked the boar.

"I don't mean to disturb you but I need your advice," blurted out Taro.

The boar walked over and looked Taro up and down. "You're too skinny. Not taking care of yourself."

"My master, the musician, wants to take me back to the mountains and leave me where he found me," cried the little monkey.

"Good," said the boar. "Humans are trouble. In my experience, I find that it's much better to keep my distance from them. It's good to go back to your own kind."

"But, I don't have any family in the mountains. I've been with the musician and his wife and child my whole life. They are the only family I know. I want to stay with them." Taro was almost in tears.

"Then tell him," the boar said impatiently.

"I try, but they doesn't understand me. They think I'm too old to dance or be of any use to them."

"If you cannot tell them you're useful, you'll have to show them. What does the musician love more than anything else?"

"He loves his son, Bokuden, more than anything."

"Good. Go back and I will take care of everything. Next time you see me, chase me."

"Chase you?" cried Taro.

The boar just nodded and returned to rooting up his supper. Taro wanted to ask more questions, but the huge boar was very intimidating and Taro could tell that the conversation was over.

The next morning, the wife woke Taro early and told him to mind the baby while she cooked the morning rice.

Taro danced and made faces for the child, but as he tried to do a cartwheel the baby reached out and grabbed his leg and they both went tumbling off the small porch and into the yard. Taro never saw the boar as it crashed through the fence and charged toward the house. The fierce animal's bristles were standing up and his red eyes blazed as he hooked his tusk in the baby's sash, turned, and began running towards the forest, with Bokuden screaming all the while.

The musician and his wife ran from the house but neither one was fast enough to catch the boar. Then Taro remembered what the boar had said and started to chase him. He could hear the musician and his wife screaming from the porch as he ran after the boar and the child. As he heard the baby crying, Taro felt something rising up from deep inside himself, a strength that the old monkey didn't know he still possessed. He found the boar and the child in a clearing. But by this time the baby was laughing and pulling on the huge boar's ears and tusks. The boar looked up and saw Taro.

"Take the child back, your future is secured," said the old boar. "The simple truth is that no one can turn a hero away from their door."

Taro took hold of the baby and started back to the house. He turned once and waved, but the boar just grunted and walked away.

The musician and his wife were crying on the steps of their porch, lamenting that they would never see their baby again, when Taro emerged from the forest with Bokuden in his arms.

"Look," cried the man, "my feeble old monkey has saved my son."

"Not so feeble or old that he could not save our son or carry him back," cried the child's mother.

She took hold of Taro and hugged him and hugged him, not wanting to let go of the old monkey, while the father held Bokuden and smiled at his old friend. Finally, the two happy parents bowed deeply to the monkey and vowed never to doubt him. They brought him inside the house, where he was given a huge bowl of morning rice. Then the musician brought Taro's bed into the house and that is where he slept from that day on.

After this, Taro and little Boduken would sometimes wander into the forest and find the old boar. There, they would sit and talk the day away, the monkey and the boy listening to the boar's stories about heroes from other times.

_____

This beautiful story reminds us of how we often take our elders for granted. Taro is obviously the hero but the boar is the wise old sage that saves the day for the snow monkey. You can find a version in Shirley Climo's book Monkey Business.

Chapter Eight

Stories for Elders

Nasrudin the Wise:
Creeping Up on Himself

Middle East

One evening, the Night watch caught Nasrudin in his garden, prying open the window of his own bedroom.

"What are you doing, Nasrudin?" asked the watchman. "Have you been locked out?"

"Quiet," whispered Nasrudin. "My family tells me I walk in my sleep. I am trying to catch myself and see if it's true."

Nasrudin the Wise:
I Know Her Too Well

Middle East

Word was sent to Nasrudin that a terrible accident had happened, his mother-in-law had fallen into the river. "I am afraid that if she is not rescued soon," said a neighbor, "she might be swept out to sea and lost forever."

Without a moment's hesitation, Nasrudin ran to the banks of the river, dove in and began to swim upstream.

"No!" cried the people on the riverbanks. "Go downstream. People are always carried downstream."

"Listen," cried Nasrudin, "I know my mother-in-law. If everyone else is carried downstream, the place to search for her is upstream."

Nasrudin the Wise:
The Value of History

Middle East

Nasrudin was sent by the king to learn about the lore and stories of various Eastern mystical teachers and scholars. Each one that he met told him stories of miracles and wonder, the wisdom of the founders and great teachers of the past. Each country he visited praised their own schools of knowledge and belittled those of other places.

When Nasrudin returned home, he sent his report to the king and it was only one word written on a page. It was the single word "carrots."

The king called him to the palace to explain his strange report. "It's quite simple," Nasrudin said. "Knowledge is like the carrot, few know by looking at the green top that the best part, the orange part, is there. Like the carrot, if you don't work for it, it will wither away and rot. And finally, like the carrot, there are a great many donkeys and jackasses that are associated with it."

Nasrudin is the Muslim everyman, a cousin to Jack. In every foolish act there is great wisdom. My friend Kathe Brinkman says that blonde jokes are the modern American version of Nasrudin. Check out the book The Exploits of the Incomparable Nasrudin *by Indries Shah and laugh till you grow wise.*

The Doctor and His Patient

Greece

There was an old woman who had become blind. A local doctor examined her and told her that, indeed, he could cure her and bring her sight back. With her neighbors as witnesses, she promised that if her sight returned she would pay the physician a substantial reward. The deal was set, and the doctor began his series of daily medications and therapy.

As he treated the old woman, the doctor noticed that she had some beautiful pieces of furniture, elegant draperies, and pieces of art that rivaled those found in any palace. Slowly, on each visit, he took a piece of furniture from that room, a painting from that wall, and some silver from that drawer, until the old woman had nothing of any value left in her home. The medications that the doctor used indeed helped the old woman, and within a few weeks, she was able to see again.

When the doctor asked for his fee, the old woman kept putting him off. Finally, he had her taken to court and there he pleaded his case.

When the judge asked her to defend herself, the woman said, "What this doctor says is true enough. I promised to pay him a handsome fee if he would restore my sight and nothing if I continued to be blind. Now, he says I am cured, but I'm not so sure. You see, your honor, before I became blind, I saw a household filled with beautiful furniture, silver, and art but, now that I am cured, I can't see any of it."

A lovely story about justice with a touch of humor. Maybe it's a good thing doctors don't make house calls any more. You can find a version in Norma Livo's book Story Medicine.

The Silent Couple

Arabia

Once, a long time ago, there was a newly wedded couple, still dressed in their rich wedding clothes, relaxing in their new home. The feast was over and the families and guests had all gone away to leave the young couple in peace and quiet.

"My dear," said the new bride, "Someone has left the front door open. Please, be my love and close it. I'm afraid the dust and noise from the street will invade our new home."

The young groom looked shocked. "You want me to shut the door? Here I am, a new bridegroom dressed in my fine clothes and wearing my jeweled dagger, and you want me to do a servant's chore? No, I will not. Go and shut it yourself."

The young bride was immediately hurt and became furious. "So, I am to be your slave? Since there are no servants here tonight, I am to do your servant's chore and close the door? I am also in my fine clothes and precious jewels adorn my neck and hands. I won't go out and close a door that leads to the street. I come from a fine family and am not used to being ordered around like this."

The two newlyweds sat quietly for a few minutes and then the young bride spoke again, "My husband, why don't we resolve this matter by making it into a game. The person who speaks first must get up and close the door." The husband nodded and they agreed to settle the argument through silence. Since there were two sofas in the room, the young bride settled into one and faced the groom as he settled into the other.

The young couple had been sitting like this for about two hours when a company of thieves walked past the entrance to the house in the darkness of the night. They saw the open door as an invitation and quietly slipped inside and began to take every item of value they could find. The young couple heard the thieves down the hall as they ransacked the house, but the wife thought that the husband should do something about it, and the husband thought his wife should, so they both sat there in stony silence like two statues.

Finally, the thieves made their way into the room where the couple sat and began to collect all of the valuables including all of the wedding presents, even the fine carpet that was in the center of the room. They finally noticed the odd couple, just sitting there speechless and quickly stripped them of their jewels and left.

All night long, the young couple sat there, acting every bit as stubborn as married couples twice their age. In the morning, the new servants came and saw that the house was open and virtually empty. They crept through the house until the servants saw the newlyweds, just sitting there, staring at each other in stony silence. The servants tried to talk to the couple, but when they did nothing but stare, the servants gave up and helped themselves to breakfast, eating and drinking coffee as if the kitchen were their own. Still, the young couple just sat there. Finally, one of the servants went out into the street and called for the police. The police officer came into the house and tried to question the young bride and groom, but to no avail. They ignored him as if he did not exist. The officer sent for his superior who came with more officers. They also tried to question the couple but the bride and groom just sat in silence, never looking left or right, but looking only straight at each other.

Finally, the senior officer lost his temper. "Give that fellow a few blows from your staff and we'll see if he'll answer us then."

One of the policemen raised his staff, but at last, the young wife could not hold herself back any longer. "Please, do not strike him. He is my husband."

The young groom leaped from the sofa, yelling, "I won! Now, get up and close the door."

What a wonderful story about a married couple that start off their life together as stubborn as can be. I wonder what they'll be like fifty years from their wedding day? Several versions are found in countries from Scotland to North America to the Middle East. There is one to be found in Idries Shah's book World Tales.

The Wise Fools of Chelm

Eastern Europe (Jewish)

One day, two of Chelm's most revered elders, Faivel and Fishel, were talking in the teahouse. Faivel had been a baker and Fishel a tailor, but now the men were retired and enjoying the great grand children that often came to see them. Faivel turned to Fishel and said, "Why do governments always tax the poor? They take our last coins."

"Governments always need money, that's why they tax us," replied Fishel.

"But they don't need our money," said Faivel. "They have their own mint where they can make as many coins as they need."

"Its just like God and angels," said Fishel.

"What do you mean, its just like God and angels?"

"I have heard that every time someone does a good deed they create an angel. God could create as many angels as he needs but he doesn't, does he? No, he'd rather have your angel. The government could create as many coins as it wants, but would rather have yours."

They both nodded at his wisdom and continued to drink their tea.

As Fishel and Faivel were slowly walking home, Fishel noticed that Faivel was carrying an umbrella, which he thought odd since the sky was blue and barely a cloud was in sight.

Suddenly, in the middle of their discussion, a terrible storm swept out of nowhere, and they were caught in the downpour.

"Quick, open your umbrella," Fishel cried. "We're getting soaked."

"It won't do any good," replied Faivel. "My umbrella is full of holes."

"Full of holes? Why did you bring it then?"

"I didn't think it would rain," replied Faivel.

In the grand tradition of Jack and Nasrudin we have these two wise fools of Chelm. Read Steve Sanfield's The Feather Merchants & Other Tales of the Fools of Chelm *for more of these delightful stories.*

The Old Woman Who Lived in a Vinegar Bottle

England

Once upon a time there was an old woman who lived in a vinegar bottle. One day as the woman sat alone in her house a fairy passed by and heard her talking to herself.

"It is a shame, a shame, a shame," said the old woman. "I shouldn't live in a vinegar bottle. I should live in a nice little cottage with a thatched roof and a garden with roses. That's where I should live." And the old woman sighed.

The fairy whispered through the window, "Very well, when you go to bed tonight turn around three times, shut your eyes, and in the morning you will see what you will see."

So the old woman went to bed, turned around three times, and shut her eyes, and in the morning she woke inside a sweet little cottage with a thatched roof and a garden and in the center of the garden there were roses. She was so surprised and so happy, but in her joy she forgot to thank the fairy.

Now the fairy traveled to the north, to the south, to the east and to the west. Soon she was near the cottage of the old woman and decided to stop in and see how she was enjoying her new home.

As she approached the front door she heard the old woman talking to herself.

"It's a shame, a shame, a shame," said the old woman. "I shouldn't be living in a cottage like this all by myself. I should live in a nice little house in a row of houses with lace at the windows, a brass knocker on my front door and happy neighbors that call out 'hello and how are you' every time we meet."

The fairy was a bit surprised, but she told the old woman, "When you go to bed turn around three times, shut your eyes and in the morning you shall see what you shall see."

So the old woman went to bed that night and she turned around three times, shut her eyes and in the morning she woke in a little house in a row of houses. There were lace curtains, a brass knocker on the front door, and all her neighbors were happy and greeted her cheerfully when she went outside. She was very surprised and very happy, but again she forgot to thank the fairy.

Now the fairy traveled to the north, to the south, to the east and to the west. Soon she was near the house of the old woman and decided to stop in and see how she was enjoying her new home. She was bound to be happy now.

When the fairy got to the row of houses and stood outside the old woman's house she heard her once more talking to herself.

"It's a shame, a shame, a shame," the old woman said. "I shouldn't live in a row of houses with common folk on all sides. I should live in a great mansion surrounded by a wonderful garden with servants to bring me this and bring me that and bring me what I need."

The fairy was surprised and a bit annoyed at this turn of events but once more she said, "Very well, go to bed tonight and turn around three times, shut your eyes and in the morning you shall see what you shall see."

The next morning the old woman woke to find that she was in a great mansion with a wonderful garden. She had servants to do her bidding and to bring her what she needed and sometimes what she didn't need. She was very surprised and delighted but she forgot to thank the fairy.

Now the fairy traveled to the north, to the south, to the east and to the west. Soon she was near the great hall of the old woman and decided to stop in and see how she was enjoying her new position in life. She had to be happy now.

No sooner had the fairy reached the window of the old woman's drawing room than she heard her talking to herself.

"It's a shame, a shame, a shame," she lamented. "I shouldn't be living here in this great house all alone. I should be a duchess or a countess and have my own coach. I should go to balls and parties with lords and ladies and even wait upon the queen."

The fairy was surprised once more by the woman's words but she told her, "When you go to bed tonight turn around three times, shut your eyes and in the morning you shall see what you shall see."

When the old woman woke she was a duchess in a fine house in London with a coach and servants and a closet full of fancy gowns. On her desk was a pile of invitations to this party and that ball and an invitation to wait upon the queen. She was very surprised and very happy but once again she forgot to thank the fairy.

Now the fairy traveled to the north, to the south, to the east and to the west. Soon she was near London and the great house of the old woman and decided to stop in and see how she was enjoying her new position in life. She had to be happy now that she was a duchess.

When she neared the window to her great dining room she heard the old woman talking to herself, "It's a shame, a shame, a shame," she cried. "Why should I have to bow to the queen? I should be queen and sit on a golden throne and the people should all bow to me."

The fairy was disappointed and a little angry but she told the old woman, "When you go to sleep tonight turn around three times, shut your eyes and in the morning you shall see what you shall see."

In the morning the old woman found herself on a golden throne with a golden crown and all the people of the kingdom bowed and called her their queen. She lived in a royal palace with all her noble ladies and gentlemen around her. She was delighted and began to order people from here to there and back again but she forgot to thank the fairy.

Now the fairy traveled to the north, to the south, to the east and to the west. Soon she was near the palace of the old woman and decided to stop in and see how she was enjoying her new position in life. She was the queen, what more could she ever want or need?

But when the fairy reached the window of the royal throne room she heard the old woman talking to herself again. "It's a shame, a shame, a shame," she cried. I am only the queen of this little country. I should be ruling the whole world. Everyone should listen to my words and obey me. I should be the empress or maybe even the pope!"

The fairy had heard quite enough. "Very well," she told the old woman. "Go to bed tonight, turn around three times and shut your eyes and in the morning you shall see what you shall see."

So the old woman, eager to rule the world, went to bed that night. She turned around three times, she shut her eyes and in the morning she was back in her vinegar bottle just where she belonged.

Some people are never satisfied. This little tale is found in many countries and involves talking fish, lime trees, and an assortment of other creatures that are always happy to give what is asked for up to a point. Amy Douglas and I have a version of this story in our book English Folktales.

The Husband Who Stayed at Home

Norway

Once a long time ago there was a husband who was always in a bad mood because he felt that he did all the work around the farm while his wife stayed home and did nothing. He was a man who could never see what was right in front of his nose.

One evening he came home complaining and telling his wife how hard his day was in the fields and how easy her life was at home.

His wife looked at him and said, "Do you think you could do the work in this house better than I?"

He laughed gruffly looking around the room. "Of course I do. Any man could do this work easily."

The wife smiled sweetly and said, "Well then, tomorrow we will trade places. I will go to the fields and work and you will stay home and do my daily chores."

Early the next day the wife put a scythe over her shoulder and went to the hayfield to mow. The husband stayed behind, planning to do her chores and have a little nap as well.

He decided to churn the butter first. After he had churned for a while he was thirsty so he went into the cellar to tap a glass of ale. He had just taken the plug out when he heard the pig grunting in the kitchen. With the tap still in his hand he ran up the cellar steps and saw that the pig had overturned the churn and was eagerly lapping up the cream.

The farmer became so angry that he chased the pig and fell face down in the cream that now had spread all over the floor. He reached out and caught the pig and hauled himself to his feet. He was so mad that he gave the pig a swift kick in the head. He kicked the pig so hard that the poor thing fell over quite dead. It was then that he looked down and saw the plug in his hand and ran down to the cellar only to see the last drop of ale fall from the barrel onto the floor.

There was still no butter for their dinner so he left the house and went to the barn in search of more cream. He skimmed off just enough to fill the churn and once more began to work. As he churned, he remembered the cow who had not been milked or taken to the pasture and had been kept in the barn all morning with no food or water. When he had milked the cow he had no time to take her to pasture because he still had to churn the butter for their dinner, clean the cream up off the floor, and butcher the dead pig. So he decided to get the cow up on the cottage roof. It slanted just a little, was covered with sod, and sat close to a steep hill. He was sure he could put a couple of planks from the hill to the roof and coax the cow over to the fine crop of waiting grass.

Just about this time, as he held the lead of the bellowing cow, he heard the baby begin to cry. Knowing it was too hungry, he didn't want to leave the churn still filled with cream in the kitchen where the baby was crawling around in search of food, so he hoisted the churn onto his back and tugged on the cow. When he managed to get the cow on the roof he remembered that the poor thing had not had any water, so he decided to get some from the well. As he bent over to pull up the bucket, all the cream from the churn went spilling over his head and into the well. He was so angry that he took the churn and threw it across the yard where it hit the side of the barn and splintered into a hundred pieces.

Now the farmer thought that since there would be no butter, and the baby was crying and no doubt covered in spilt cream, and he had not even started dinner, that he had better at least make some porridge. He hurried back into the kitchen, stepping over the dead pig and trying not to slip in puddles of cream. He grabbed the soaking, screaming baby up, filled a pot with water, and put it over the fire to boil. It was at that point that he heard the cow above and remembered that he had failed to tie her to a tether. What if she fell off and broke her leg? What would he do then?

He dropped the baby and ran to the barn where he grabbed a length of rope. He climbed up on the roof again, tied the rope around the cow's neck, and then hung the rope down the chimney so he could tie it to something solid in the kitchen.

When he returned to the kitchen he saw the water boiling and threw some oatmeal into the pot. The baby, still crying, was crawling near the fire. The husband hurriedly wrapped the rope around his ankle so he could pick up the baby and put him back into his cradle. With the baby screaming in the cradle, the man went back to the fireplace to stir the porridge, which bubbled over and down into the fire. At this moment, the cow fell off the roof and the man was pulled halfway up the chimney, dangling by his ankle, above the overturned porridge and the smoking fire. It was then that his wife came home.

Now, the wife had had a fine day mowing and had cut down seven lengths and seven breadths of the field. She had expected her husband to call her to dinner, but when no call had come she decided to return home.

When the wife arrived in the barnyard she saw the broken butter churn and the cow dangling near the ground, hanging from the roof of the house. She ran up and took her scythe and cut the rope so the cow could be freed. This caused her husband to come falling down the chimney face first into the spilt porridge and dying fire. The wife rushed into the house past the dead pig, over the floor smeared with cream, up to her crying baby, and her poor husband groaning in the fireplace.

In silence the husband and the wife cleaned up the baby and the house, hung the pig up to be butchered, and put the cow out to pasture. As the wife comforted the baby, they sat down to a meager dinner of stale bread without butter, porridge, or ale.

Soon, the wife turned to her husband and smiled. "No matter dear. Tomorrow is another day and I'm sure you'll get the hang of running the house."

The husband held his aching head and slowly chewed his bread. "I think that I am better suited to the simple task of farming and that the work of a woman can only be done by a woman," he said.

That night, when together in bed, the husband and wife laughed about his misadventures and the farmer never again complained about his work or how easy it must be for his wife to keep the house.

The pitfalls of role reversal! This delightful story can be found in many cultures. Two versions that I particularly like are those found in East of the Sun, West of the Moon *by George Webbe Dasent and* The Maid of the North *by Ethel Johnston Phelps.*

Solomon's Magic Ring

Israel

One of King Solomon's most trusted advisers was the captain of his guard, Benaiah. A quiet man, he was devoted to the king and his love for Solomon was well known to all. One day, King Solomon overheard Benaiah talking to some other advisers in the palace. He was boasting that the king had never given him an assignment that he did not finish, a task he did not accomplish fully. The king was both annoyed and amused at Benaiah's uncharacteristic bragging. Solomon decided to give his captain an impossible assignment.

The next day the king called Benaiah into the throne room. "I wish for you to find me a magical ring, one I have heard tales about," the king said. "It is a ring that can make a happy man sad and a sad man happy, a ring that can make a poor man smile and a rich man frown. I wish to have this ring as my own."

"If it is your wish, my king," replied Benaiah, "then I will not rest until I bring this ring to you."

As his friend left the throne room, Solomon smiled at the thought of Benaiah searching for a ring that did not exist.

Benaiah went to the market in Jerusalem and inquired from every goldsmith, every silver smith, every trader and merchant, but no one had ever heard of such a magical ring. He left Jerusalem and traveled to other cities, other countries. Whenever he stopped at an oasis, he asked every caravan leader and soldier of fortune that he met, but none had ever heard of the fabled ring. He traveled to ports on the sea and towns on the banks of great rivers, and asked those who sailed upon the water if they had heard of such a ring but none had ever heard even a whisper about it. Benaiah asked wise men and seers, wizards and noted scholars but none could help him with his search. The weeks turned to months, the months turned to years, and still Benaiah searched on. He sold his fine cloak and tunic, his sword and jeweled dagger, to support him in his quest.

King Solomon regretted sending his trusted friend on a fool's mission. He sent others to look for his captain, but they could have walked right past Benaiah and not known him at all. His hair and beard were long and matted. The sun had burnt his face and hands until they had turned black. He no longer looked like the adviser to a king but more like a beggar, making his journey through life.

Finally, Benaiah's travels brought him back to Jerusalem. As he approached the gate to the city, wondering how he could face his king and admit his failure, he began to weep. An old man walking next to him looked over at his face and said, "My friend, you seem so very sad. What is it that worries you?"

Benaiah told him about his years away from Jerusalem and his search for a ring that he could not find.

The old man smiled and said, "I have such a ring. Please, take it if it will bring you some happiness." The old man reached into his coat and produced a simple gold ring and handed it to the wanderer. Benaiah took it and read the inscription that circled the ring. Filled with gratitude, he smiled, thanked the man, and walked straight to Solomon's court.

When Solomon saw Benaiah walking toward his throne, he stepped down and held his arms out to his old friend. Tears welled in the king's eyes as he saw how Benaiah had changed over the years of his search. Solomon was just about to tell him how sorry he was for having sent Benaiah on such an impossible mission, one that offered no hope of success, when Benaiah dropped to his knees, looked up at Solomon, and smiled.

"My king," said Benaiah, "I have wandered and searched and have finally found that which you sent me to bring you all those years ago." Benaiah extended his hand toward Solomon and opened it. The king looked down at the small gold band that lay there in his friend's palm. Taking the ring, the king read the inscription. When he looked up and cast his eyes around his throne room, and down at his jeweled hands and his fine clothes, his smile faded. He called for one of his guards to bring an old beggar man that had just walked past the palace gate to the throne room. As soon as the frightened old man walked into the palace, Solomon handed him the ring. The man's tired, worn-out face broke into a smile as he read the words on the ring. The king took the ring back, exchanging it for a bag of gold, and sent the grateful beggar on his way.

Solomon gave one of the jeweled rings he wore that day to Benaiah and slipped the small gold band on his own finger. He never took it off. The words inscribed on the ring that could make a rich man frown and a poor man smile were "Gam Zeh Ya'avor," This Too Shall Pass. Solomon always kept those words in his heart and the ring on his finger. After all, it was a magic ring.

What a remarkable story. It is found in many traditions including Sufi. I enjoy the telling of it in Heather Forest's book Wisdom Tales.

Using the Book with School Children

This book shows elders in various situations from heroic to foolish. It is important for children to see their elders in this light, as humans with strengths and faults, and still maintain their admiration and respect for them.

Reading the stories is the simplest way to share them, but that isn't the end of their usefulness in the classroom.

Collecting Stories from Elders in Their Own Families

After reading several stories from the book, begin to ask students if they have heard any old stories from older family members or if their parents learned any stories from their own parents and relatives. Remember to use the term "old stories" rather then "traditional stories" or "folktales." Most people would say no, they hadn't heard folktales as a child but will say that they learned old stories from family members. As a boy, I learned dozens of traditional folktales that my Grandmother had brought to America with her when she came from Croatia, but I always heard them referred to as "old stories" or as stories she learned from her mother or father or village stories. The concept of the folktale is more academic and doesn't usually find a place in the vocabulary of the family storyteller. Have the students include jokes and recipes in their collecting. Often people will start out by telling you a recipe, as they explain the ingredients to the listener, will then launch into the story of how they learned to make the dish. One thing does lead to another.

When teaching students how to conduct an interview, you can play a game with them that will teach them what kind of questions to ask. I have them pretend they are interviewing me and that I am a character from a famous fairy tale or movie. They need to discover my identity by asking me questions (not my name or character or the name of the story or movie) that will lead to my name. The questions cannot be answered by a yes or a no. If the students do ask a yes or no question they get points deducted from their score—two points for a good question but a minus five for a yes or no question. The game quickly teaches them to ask questions that will lead to a narrative answer, and that might lead to a story.

Collecting Stories in the Community

Using the same methods outlined above, students can collect stories of their community at senior centers, community centers, retirement homes, and nursing homes. With the same interviewing techniques, students can record stories in these different environments that will help them understand the historical and ethnic backgrounds of their area.

To break the ice, I would suggest that the students work in teams of two or three students and that they begin their collecting with a performance for the residents or people in attendance in which they sing a few songs or recite some poetry or tell a few stories. In this way, there is an exchange between the interviewer and the subject that is less one-sided. It also introduces the students to the people they are going to interview in a nonthreatening way.

These stories can also be collected on tape or in book form and donated to the nursing home or senior center. A copy should also be in both the school and public library.

Sample Questions to Ask

On the following page are a few questions that should help "prime the pump" during an interview. Always remember to get their name, address, where they were raised, and the year they were born on the tape before you start asking questions.

1. Could you tell me about what school was like when you were a child? Did you have a favorite teacher?

2. Could you tell me about some of your favorite games that you played? (If the games are unfamiliar to you, ask the person you are interviewing to explain the rules.)

3. What was your neighborhood like? (If the person grew up in a rural setting, ask him or her about the farm and the nearest town that he or she would visit.)

4. Did you have any pets? Can you tell me about them?

5. What was your favorite holiday when you were a child?

6. What did you do during the war? (This pertains to people in who are in their eighties and older, people who were young adults during the World War II era.)

7. What did you do for a living? Did you enjoy it? Where did you learn your skill?

8. Did you marry? Did you have children? Tell me about your family.

9. Do you remember any stories you heard as a child?

10. Did you have brothers or sisters? Did you get along? Tell me about some of the things you did together.

Often times, just a few questions open a floodgate of memories. Tell the students to be prepared to let the person they're interviewing just talk. Their listening might be the most important thing to happen to them in quite a while.

Alternative Endings, Alternative Viewpoints

Have students pick a story and then write an alternative ending that will show a different side of the elder character in the story. For example, if in the story "The Wise Woman" her ruse hadn't worked, what would have happened to her and the people of her city? Or in "The Thief," what would have happened if one of the people the thief gave the seed to actually proved to be an honest person? What would happen to the Geats if Beowulf failed to kill the dragon?

By having the students rewrite the endings, they get to explore other aspects of both the story and the character of elders in the story.

Another exercise is to have the students rewrite the stories from a different point of view. For example, tell the story of Beowulf from the dragon's point of view. Why did he attack the Geats? How does he view the world of men? Tell the story of Rose Red from Molo's point of view. Why did he help his young master? Did he feel betrayed at the end? In the "Mocker Mocked," tell the story from the old woman's point of view. How did she feel being called names and ridiculed? Or tell the same story from the wife's point of view. Why did this happen to me? How does she see life now that she is no longer beautiful?

Questions for Discussion

Here is a sample of questions that can be used for classroom discussions about elders. The stories can be read out loud, and then the various topics can be discussed in class or by written assignment.

The Thief

In this story we find an old thief who uses his cunning and wits to get out of prison.

1. Is the thief any less guilty than the king and his ministers? Why or why not?
2. Was the seed actually magic?
3. What crimes did the king commit that kept him from making the tree grow?
4. Do we see this type of crime today?

The Wise Woman

This story involves wisdom that can save a whole city from destruction.

1. In this story, the people did not want to trust the elder right away. Why not?

2. What were the people hiding that the wise woman needed to save them?

3. What was she trying to prove to the army laying siege to her city?

4. Why was she wise? What did she know about her people and the enemy?

The Witch of Kamalalaya

This is a story about how people distrust those they do not understand.

1. Was the wise woman of this story a witch? Why or why not?

2. What did she know that made the people fear her?

3. Why did the children taunt her, and why did folks distrust her?

4. What did she use to save the lost sheep?

5. What lesson did the young shepherd learn?

6. Have you ever called someone names or been mean to them only because you didn't know them or understand them or because they were different? Is that right?

The Father Who Went to School

The sons and daughters-in-law in this story want to get rid of the father. He has given them his land and money, but now he is a burden.

1. Why did they want their father to go to school?

2. When he came back with the box, why did they suddenly become nice to him?

3. Did the children deserve any reward after he died? Why or why not?

4. Should children take care of their parents when they become too old to take care of themselves?

The Wooden Bowl

In this story, the parents of the little boy treat the grandfather poorly. The grandson comes to his aid.

1. What did the grandfather do to deserve the punishment he received?

2. How did the grandson help make his parents understand what they were doing?

3. What did the wooden bowl represent?

4. Would you do the same for one of your grandparents? Why?

5. Who was the hero of this story?

I'll Roast You and I'll Toast You

The old woman in this story frightens off the robbers, but she never knows that she did.

1. Why was the old woman talking to her kippers?

2. Why did the robbers think she was talking about them?

3. Do you know people who talk to themselves? Has it ever frightened you? Why?

4. What was happening to the robbers when they heard the old woman talking?

The Old Traveler

In this story, an old traveler gives two different households two very different gifts.

1. Why did the first woman chase the old man from her door?

2. Why did the second woman let him stay?

3. The poor woman and her children shared their home, and the little boy shared his bed. Why did these poor people do that?

4. What was the gift that the old traveler gave the poor family, and how did it change their lives?

5. Why was the mean woman suddenly nice to the old man?

6. What was the gift he gave the second woman, and how did it change her life?

7. How should we treat others?

The Bremen Town Musicians

This is a well-known story about growing old, and how animals (and sometimes people) are discarded when they are worth saving.

1. Why did the animals leave their farms?

2. How did the animals become friends?

3. How did they think they would make a living in Bremen Town?

4. Why were the thieves afraid when the animals first came into the house?

5. Why did the young thief think the animals were something else when he returned?

6. Does becoming old mean that you are useless? What did the heroes of this story prove about old age?

The Monkey and the Boar

In this story the monkey is an orphan, and the musician and his wife adopt him.

1. How does the monkey help the musician?
2. Why does the monkey take care of the baby?
3. Why does the musician want to get rid of the monkey? What will he do with him?
4. Why does the monkey want to stay?
5. Does the boar help? How?
6. Why do they let Taro stay?

The Husband Who Stayed at Home

Here we have a story about two people exchanging jobs for a day.

1. Did the husband have an easy time doing his wife's work? Why or why not?
2. Did the wife enjoy doing her husband's work?
3. What lesson did the husband learn?
4. Have you ever tried to do someone else's job and find out that it was more difficult than you thought? What job was it?

Using the Book with Elders

The stories in this book are meant not only to showcase tales that have been handed down through the centuries about our elders but also to be enjoyed and used by elders themselves. The section "Stories for Elders" is for their enjoyment and amusement, but there are stories in each chapter that are there to make elders laugh, cry, or just wonder about. Here are some sample questions that you can use to guide your group in discussions.

Humor

In stories such as "Creeping Up on Himself," we are introduced to Nasrudin, the wise fool of the Muslim people. He is all fun and foolishness, although he also expresses wisdom in his seemingly crazy words.

Questions to discuss:

1. How is wisdom expressed through humor different from other forms of wisdom?
2. Have you ever known someone like Nasrudin?
3. Are you at all like Nasrudin? In what ways?
4. Do you have a favorite joke or humorous saying you'd like to share?

Relationships

In "Baucis and Philemon," we talk about love and devotion to a spouse. In this story, they seem to enjoy the next world together.

Questions to discuss:

1. Have you ever known a couple like Baucis and Philemon? Tell us a story about them.
2. It is apparent that Baucis and Philemon loved each other deeply. Do you think this kind of love is rare? Why or why not?
3. Does anyone know a love story they would like to share?

In the stories "The Husband Who Stayed at Home" and "The Silent Couple," we find two different problems that might arise in a marriage.

Questions to discuss:

1. Are you ever stubborn like the silent couple?
2. Tell us a story about a time you were stubborn. What finally happened?
3. Did you ever switch roles with your spouse? Why did you do this?
4. Did you appreciate his or her work more or less when you switched roles? What did you learn from the experience?

In the story "The Grandfather and His Grandson," it seems that no matter what the man does, he's criticized for it.

Questions to discuss:

1. Have you ever felt that no matter what you did, others thought you were in the wrong? Tell us about it?
2. Have you ever been with a grandchild or someone much younger than yourself and experienced something that you were able to laugh about together—and even learn something from? Tell us about it.
3. What lesson did the boy learn from his grandfather on the day recalled in the story? Do you think that the grandfather might have planned the whole thing? Why?

In the stories "The Wooden Bowl" and "The Magic Forest," the elder in the family is treated badly. In both they are finally rescued.

Questions to discuss:

1. How could the abuse have been stopped earlier in these stories?
2. Should or could the older character have done something sooner? What?
3. Have you ever known anyone who experienced abuse at the hands of a child, a spouse, or a caregiver? What happened?
4. How can we stop elder abuse in our society?

Wisdom

In many folktales, the elder is considered a source of wisdom. Stories such as "The Wise Woman," "The Doll That Caught a Thief," and "The King and the Peasant" illustrate the wisdom of elders.

Questions to discuss:

1. How does wisdom come with age?
2. What makes wisdom so important in our society, especially among elders?
3. Does advanced age help people when they speak up about an issue? Why or why not?
4. Have you ever been able to use the knowledge you've gained over the years to help someone? Tell us about this experience.
5. Was there someone in your family as you were growing up who was wise and shared that wisdom with others? Tell us about that person.
6. Do you think that wisdom is still honored in today's society?

Foolishness

Wisdom is not the only thing that comes with age. In the stories "The Lion's Share" and "A Debate in Sign Language," the characters are not very wise. In the end, one becomes a hero, and the other gets away with his skin.

Questions to discuss:

1. Have you ever had an experience like the one in "A Debate in Sign Language," that is, a time when you misunderstood someone, but it turned out all right in the end? Tell us about it.
2. In "The Lion's Share," the elder of the pack is not only foolish but also a bit of a braggart. Have you ever known someone who has bragged about something, only to back down later? Tell us about it.

3. Have you ever known someone who was just plain foolish? Tell us a story about that person.

4. Why do we love to laugh at the mistakes of others? Do you laugh at your own?

Justice

In the stories "The Crane's Purse," "The Widow and the Fishes," and "The Old Traveler," people get what they deserve by the end of the story.

1. Do people always get their just rewards in the end? Why or why not?

2. Were you ever involved in something that caused someone else to get what he or she deserved? Tell us about it.

3. Why is justice so important in life?

4. Why is it so satisfying to watch as someone who has not been quite fair gets his or her comeuppance?

This Too Shall Pass

In the wonderful tale "Solomon's Magic Ring," we have that great line: "this too shall pass." The story gives us a warning and a blessing all at the same time.

1. What do you think "this too shall pass" means?

2. Have you had moments when you needed this phrase in your life? Tell us about such an experience.

3. Benaiah was so loyal to Solomon. Have you ever known a person like him in your life? How did he or she show loyalty?

4. What was going on in Solomon's mind when he read those words? In the beggar's mind?

Telling a Story

Let someone from your group tell a story that's in the book or one remembered from his or her own past. Have storytelling become a time when people feel safe, whether in the audience or on stage. The story session should be a time that people look forward to and are eager to listen, share, or both. Be prepared to hear the same stories over and over again. Remember, they get richer with each telling. Never ask for folktales or fairy tales; the first one has no meaning for most people, and the latter is associated more commonly with children. Ask for "any old story"—stories they learned as children, or true stories that come from their own lives. Icebreaking topics include pets, school, children, marriage, war exploits, and occupations.

Using the Stories as a Starting Place

By reading the stories, elders can identify with characters and situations that will trigger memories from their own past. These memories can be used to write the stories of their lives in books journals. They can also be recorded electronically for the tellers' children, grandchildren, neighbors, and friends, as well as future generations in the community, to read and use as a time capsules that give insight into a community's past. Copies should be given not only to family members, but also to public and school libraries.

Bibliography and Further Reading

About Storytelling, Folktales, and Elders

Family Tales, Family Wisdom; How to Gather the Stories of a Lifetime & Share Them with Your Family; Dr. Robert U. Akeret, William Morrow & Company, ISBN 0-688-10177-1

Spinning Tales, Weaving Hope: Stories, Storytelling & Activities for Peace, Justice & the Environment; Ed Brody, Jay Goldspinner, Katie Green, Rona Leventhal & John Porcino, New Society Publishers, ISBN 0-86571-447-9

Beyond the Hero: Classic Stories of Men in Search of Soul; Allan B. Chinen, Tarcher/Putnam Book, ISBN 0-87477-737-2

In the Ever After: Fairy Tales & the Second Half of Life; Allan B. Chinen, Chiron, ISBN 0-933029-41-1

Once Upon a Midlife: Classic Stories & Mythic Tales to Illuminate the Middle Years; Allan B. Chinen, Tarcher/Putnam Book, ISBN 0-87477-725-9

Spinning Straw into Gold: What Fairy Tales Reveal about the Transformations in a Woman's Life; Joan Gould, Random House, ISBN 0-394-58532-1

Storytelling Folklore Sourcebook; Norma J. Livo & Sandra A. Rietz, Libraries Unlimited, ISBN 0-87287-601-2

The Storyteller's Start-Up Book: Finding, Learning, Performing and Using Folktales; Margaret Read MacDonald, August House, ISBN 0-87483-305-1

Listening to Old Voices: Folklore, Life Stories, & the Elderly; Patrick B. Mullen, University of Illinois Press, ISBN 0-252-01808-7

The Family Storytelling Handbook; Anne Pellowski, MacMillan, ISBN 0-02-770610-9

No Go the Bogeyman: Scaring, Lulling & Making Mock; Marina Warner, Farrar, Straus & Giroux, ISBN 0-374-22301-7

Collections

Brazilian Folktales; Livia de Almeida and Ana Portella; Libraries Unlimited, ISBN 1-56308-930-0

The Lion's Whisker & Other Ethiopian Tales; Brent Ashabranner & Russell Davis, Linnet Books, ISBN 0-208-02429-8

Wise Women: Folk and Fairy Tales from Around the World; retold by Suzanne I. Barchers, Libraries Unlimited, ISBN 0-87287-816-3

A Dictionary of British Folktales in the English Language, Parts A & B; Katherine Briggs, Routledge, ISBN 0-415-06696-4 (for the two-volume set)

Happily Ever After: Folktales That Illuminate Marriage & Commitment; Meliss Bunce, August House, ISBN 0-87483-674-3

Arab Folktales; Inea Bushnaq, Pantheon Books, ISBN 0-394-50104-7

Tales of a Basque Grandmother; Frances Carpenter, Amereon House

Greedy Mariani & Other Folktales of the Antilles; Dorothy Sharp Carter, Margaret K. McElderry Books, ISBN 0-689-30425-0

Legends of the World; edited by Richard Cavendish, Schocken Books, ISBN 0-8053805-0

World Folktales; Atelia Clarkson & Gilbert B. Cross, Charles Scribner's Sons, ISBN 0-684-16290-3

Monkey Business: Stories from Around the World; Shirley Climo, Henry Holt, ISBN 0-8050-6392-7

Best Loved Folktales of the World; Joanna Cole, Anchor Press; ISBN 0-385-18949-4

Tricks of Women & Other Albanian Tales; Paul Fenimore Cooper, William Morrow, 1928

Ride with the Sun: An Anthology of Folk Tales and Stories from the United Nations; edited by Harold Courlander, McGraw-Hill, 1955

The Healing Heart—Communities; Allison M. Cox & David H. Albert, New Society, ISBN 0-86571-469-X

The Healing Heart—Families; Allison M. Cox & David H. Albert, New Society, ISBN 0-86571-467-3

In Full Bloom: Tales of Women in Their Prime; Sharon Creeden, August House, ISBN 0-87483-576-3

East of the Sun & West of the Moon; George Webbe Dasent, Dover Books, ISBN 486-22521-6

Legends & Folk Tales of Holland; told by Adele de Leeuw, Hippocrene Books, ISBN 0-7818-0743-3

Armenian Folktales & Fables; Charles Downing, Oxford University Press, ISBN 0-19-274155-1

Folk Tales from Portugal; Alan Feinstein, A.S. Barnes, ISBN 0-498-01031-7

Stories of the Spirit, Stories of the Heart: Parables of the Spiritual Path from Around the World; Christina Feldman & Jack Kornfield, HarperCollins, ISBN 0-06-250300-6

Greek Myths & Legends; Diana Ferguson, Collins & Brown, ISBN 1-85585-766-9

Musings: Tales of Truth & Wisdom; Linda M. Ford, Fulcrum, ISBN 1-55591-980-4

Wisdom Tales from Around the World; Heather Forest, August House, ISBN 0-87483-478-3

Folk Tales of the British Isles; Michael Foss, Book Club Associates, 1977

Korean Folk &Fairy Tales; Suzanne Crowder Han, Hollym International, ISBN 0-930878-04-3

Favorite Children's Stories from China & Tibet; Lotta Carswell Hume, Charles E. Tuttle Co., ISBN 0-8048-1605-0

English Folktales; Dan Keding & Amy Douglas, Libraries Unlimited, ISBN 1-59158-260-1

Stories of Hope & Spirit: Folktales from Eastern Europe; Dan Keding, August House, ISBN 0-87483-727-8

Moon Cakes to Maize: Delicious World Folktales; Norma J. Livo, Fulcrum, ISBN 1-55591-973-1

Story Medicine: Multicultural Tales of Healing & Transformation; Norma J. Livo, Libraries Unlimited, ISBN1-56308-894-0

Three Minute Tales: Stories from Around the World to Tell or Read When Time Is Short; Margaret Read MacDonald, August House, ISBN 0-87483-728-6

Dragons, Ogres, and Wicked Witches; Milos Maly, Gallery Books, ISBN 0-8317-2456-0

Why Monkeys Live in Trees and Other Stories from Benin; Raouf Mama. Curbstone Press, ISBN 1-931896-21-6

Sir Green Hat & the Wizard; Ruth Manning-Sanders, Methuen Children's Books, ISBN 416-77900-X

Bullfinch's Mythology; edited by Richard Martin, HarperCollins, ISBN 0-06-270025-1

Tales from the Heart of the Balkans; Bonnie C. Marshall, Libraries Unlimited, ISBN 1-56308-870-3

Folktales of Greece; edited by Georgios A. Megas, University of Chicago Press, ISBN 0-226-51786-1

Folktales of Israel, Dov Noy, University of Chicago Press, 1963

The Tales of India; Daulat Pandy, Sri Aurobindo Ashram, India, 1963

The Maid of the North; Ethel Johnston Phelps, Holt, Rinehart & Winston, ISBN 0-03-056893-5

The Merry Frogs; Idella Purnell, Suttonhouse, 1936

Outfoxing Fear; Kathleen Ragan, W. W. Norton, ISBN 0-393-06036-5

Zen Flesh, Zen Bones; Paul Reps, Charles E. Tuttle, ISBN 0-8048-0644-6

The Red King and the Witch; Ruth Manning-Sanders; Oxford University Press, 1964

The Feather Merchants & Other Tales of the Fools of Chelm; Steve Sanfield, Orchard Books, ISBN 0-531-05958-8

Folktales of Japan; Keigo Seki, University of Chicago Press, 1963

The Exploits of the Incomparable Mulla Nasrudin; Indries Shah, Simon & Schuster, 1966

World Tales; Indries Shah, Octagon Press, ISBN 0-86304-036-5

Korean Children's Favorite Stories; Kim So-un, Tuttle, ISBN 0-8048-3591-8

The Fairy Tale Tree; Vladislav Stanovsky and Jan Vladislav, G. P. Putnam & Sons, 1961

Tales of the Punjab; collected by Annie Steel, Bodley Head, ISBN 0-370-01271-2

The Magic Egg & Other Tales from Ukraine; Barbara J. Suwyn, Libraries Unlimited, ISBN 1-56308-425-2

The Magic Crocodile & Other Folktales from Indonesia; Alice M. Terada, University of Hawaii Press, ISBN 0-8248-1654-4

Tortoise the Trickster and Other Tales from Cameroon; Loreto Todd, Routledge & Kegan Paul, ISBN 0-7102-0740-9

Yiddish Folktales; Beatrice Silverman Weinreich, Schocken Books, ISBN 0-8052-1090-3

The Chinese Fairy Book; edited by R. Wilhelm, Frederick A. Stokes, 1921 [out of print]

Legends and Folklore of Viet Nam; Tam Dang Wei, Urbana, Illinois, self-published

Favorite Folktales from Around the World; Jane Yolen, Pantheon Books, ISBN 0-394-54382-3

Gray Heroes: Elder Tales from Around the World; Jane Yolen, Penguin Books, ISBN 0-14-027618-1

Mirror, Mirror: Forty Folktales for Mothers & Daughters to Share; Jane Yolen & Heidi E. Y. Stemple, Viking, ISBN 0-670-88907-5

The Complete Fairy Tales of the Brothers Grimm; translated by Jack Zipes; Bantam Books, ISBN 0-553-05184-9

A Mountain of Gems: Fairy Tales of the Peoples of the Soviet; (no author given), Raduga, 1975

Index

About the Author

DAN KEDING (www.dankeding.com) is an internationally recognized storyteller. He has performed at some of the most prestigious storytelling events in the world including The National Storytelling Festival in Jonesborough, Tennessee; The Festival at the Edge in Much Wenlock, England, The Timpanogos Storytelling Festival in Orem, Utah and over four hundred other festivals. He is a sought after workshop and master class leader and has appeared at The National Storytelling Conference four times, The Society for Storytelling Conference in England, The International Storytelling Institute at East Tennessee State University, and has been a guest lecturer at The University of Illinois in Urbana/Champaign. His recordings have won The American Library Association Notable Recording for Children Award and six Storytelling World Awards. His first book "Stories of Hope and Spirit" won the prestigious Anne Izard Storytellers' Choice Award and a Storytelling World Award while his second book, "English Folktales" coauthored with Amy Douglas won a Storytelling World Award. In 2000 Dan was inducted into The National Storytelling Networks Circle of Excellence. He has been a regular columnist for Sing Out! The Folk Music Magazine for twenty years. Dan continues to perform. He lives in Urbana, Illinois with his wife Tandy Lacy and their two Australian Shepherds, Jack and Maeve.